Jesus said, "...this kind does not go out except by prayer and fasting." (Matthew 17:21)

Experience the Power, Blessings and Benefits of Biblical

PRAYER
—— AND ——
FASTING

CHRISTIAN DAMANKA

Unless otherwise indicated, all Scripture quotations are from the
Holy Bible, King James Version (KJV)
All Scripture quotations marked (NKJV) are from New King James Version.
All Scripture quotations marked (AMP) are from Amplified Bible.
All Scripture quotations marked (AMPC) are from Amplified Bible, Classic Edition
All Scripture quotations marked (GNT) are from Good News Translation.
All Scripture quotations marked (NIV) are from New International Version.
All Scripture quotations marked (MSG) are from The Message Bible.
All Scripture quotations marked (NLT) are from New Living Translation.

**Experience the Power, Blessings and Benefits of
Biblical Prayer and Fasting**
ISBN 978-1-907295-16-4
© Revealed Series by Christian Damanka

Original Manuscript typed by Christian Damanka
Request for further information be addressed to the author:
Email: crissdam18@gmail.com

Published By: DUAL EDGE INC.

Dual Edge Inc.

All Rights Reserved.
No part of this publication may be reproduced, stored in a retrieval system or transmitted in any form or by any means, electronic, mechanical, photocopying, recording or otherwise, without prior written permission of the Publisher.

Typesetting, Page layout & Cover Design by
Kafui Afenyo (www.kafmedia.com)

Printed in United Kingdom

Dedication

To:

Pastor James & Pastor-Mrs Florence Ibitoye. You've been a blessing to me and to the Work of God these many years. Your Love for God, your Humility, Loyalty, Dedication and Commitment to the Work of God is amazing. Thank you.

Deacon Sylvester & Deaconess-Mrs Hannah Osei Agyemang. Am grateful for Your Great Support all these Years. Keep up the good work of the Lord.

All Global Intercessors and Prayer Warriors.

"…pray ye therefore the Lord of the harvest, that He would send forth labourers into His harvest." (Luke 10:2)

God's Prophetic Promise

"Now, therefore," says the Lord, "Turn to Me with all your heart, With fasting, with weeping, and with mourning."

So rend your heart, and not your garments; Return to the Lord your God, For He is gracious and merciful, Slow to anger, and of great kindness; And He relents from doing harm.

Who knows if He will turn and relent, And leave a blessing behind Him… Consecrate a fast, Call a sacred assembly;

"So I will restore to you the years that the swarming locust has eaten, The crawling locust, The consuming locust, And the chewing locust, My great army which I sent among you.

You shall eat in plenty and be satisfied, And praise the name of the Lord your God, Who has dealt wondrously with you; And My people shall never be put to shame.

Then you shall know that I am in the midst of Israel: I am the Lord your God And there is no other. My people shall never be put to shame."

Joel 2:12-15, 25-27 (NKJV)

Contents

Dedication		iii
God's Prophetic Promise		v
Introduction		ix
1	What is Prayer?	15
2	56 Reasons Why You Must Pray	25
3	4 Main Aspects of Biblical Prayer	75
4	When To Pray	83
5	How To Pray	89
6	Things To Pray For	119
7	Biblical Conditions for Effective Fervent Prayer	135
8	What is Fasting?	151
9	What is Biblical Fasting?	155
10	Types of Fasts	163
11	Kinds of Fasts	165
12	The Purpose of Fasting	177
13	Things to Expect During Fasting	181
14	23 Reasons Why You Should Fast	189
15	How Long Should a Person Fast?	255
16	How to Start Your Fasting	259

17	Basic Ingredients of Biblical Fasting	265
18	The Wrong Kind of Fasting	275
19	The Right Kind of Fasting	279
20	20 Great Lessons In Biblical Fasting	283
21	Who Should Fast?	287
22	How to Break Your Fast	291
Bibliography		295
Other Books by the Author		297
About the Author		299

Introduction

In my early years as a Christian, I had a thorough teaching on Prayer and Fasting from my Pastor, Rt. Rev. Dr. Emmanuel K. Gbordzoe, who was then the Head Pastor of Ho-Fiave E. P. Church of Ghana, now Global Evangelical Church. This was followed by other relevant lessons on Prayer and Fasting which I learned through Scripture Union (SU), Youth For Christ (YFC), and by researching and reading a selection of good Christian literature for the purpose of acquisition of knowledge and good practice in following the steps of Christ by Praying and Fasting in a biblical way. This was one of my passions.

I have strictly, passionately and practically followed these teachings throughout my Christian life and in my walk with the Lord, and I have gladly enjoyed, received and experienced tremendous blessings and benefits from employing the biblical Fasting-Prayer. With this background, I strictly observed Fasting and Prayer.

However, I have observed that many people are ignorant of the truth about biblical principles of Prayer and Fasting. For this reason, people spend much time praying and fasting – for months, weeks, and days, and they are worryingly surprised that they do not get the desired results or receive the desired answers from the God of heaven.

I humbly suggest to you that sometimes (**not in all cases**), we do not receive answers because we may have fasted and prayed wrongly (in an **un-biblical way**). *The Bible clearly teaches us that there is the Right and Wrong Way to Fast and Pray* (Isaiah 58; Matthew 6). That is what this amazing and unique book is about.

Prayer is a way of communicating with a supreme being. People of various faith groups and all religions pray to a particular deity, god or supreme being in one form or another, in one way or another, "*…and yet I show you a more excellent way" (1 Corinthians 12:31 NKJV)*, in this book, with the help of the Holy Spirit.

- Prayerlessness renders a believer weak spiritually (Ephesians 6:10).
- The lack of prayer in the life of a child of God makes him or her vulnerable, unproductive and ineffective spiritually and physically (Ephesians 6:10).
- A prayerless believer will be unable to withstand the wiles of the devil (Ephesians 6:11).
- A prayerless believer is powerless against the forces of darkness and the agents of the devil (Ephesians 6:12).

- A prayerless believer is unable to withstand in the evil day, and less able to stand steadfast in the faith (Ephesians 6:12).
- The prayer-closet is our place of spiritual renewal, spiritual strength and spiritual empowerment (Ephesians 6:12).

Fasting is a spiritual exercise just like Prayer. The period of fasting is also a time of cleansing whereby the life of Christ and the grace gifts of God are released upon you, stirred up in you, and made manifest in your life by the power of the Holy Spirit, to bless people, touch lives for Christ, edify the body of Christ, and promote God's Kingdom Business (GKB) on earth till Jesus comes to rapture the church.

Prayer and Fasting are biblical principles taught by Jesus Christ by word as well as action through His personal example. Jesus Himself fasted and prayed (Matthew 4:1-2; Luke 4:1-2).

Jesus' teaching clearly indicates that He expects all children of God to fast. He said, **"When you fast,"** Not if you fast.

In Matthew 6:16ff, Jesus said, "...*when ye fast, be not, as the hypocrites, of a sad countenance: for they disfigure their faces, that they may appear unto men to fast. Verily I say unto you, They have their reward. But thou,* **when thou fastest***, anoint thine head, and wash thy face; That thou appear not unto men to fast, but unto* *thy Father which is in secret: and thy Father, which seeth in secret, shall reward thee openly"* (**Matthew 6:16-18**).

Biblical prayer and fasting should never be directed to a human being, rather, it should be a ministry to God out of a heart full of love, worship and thanksgiving. There is a right and wrong way to fast according to Jesus Christ's teaching in **Matthew chapter 6**.

A number of Believers make excuses for not fasting and praying, however, those excuses remain excuses and God's word still remain the same. Believers who make up excuses for not fasting and praying are the ones who need it most.

Biblical prayer and fasting is an act of obedience to God. Though staying voluntarily without food may make a person become hungry, you must tune your mind from the flesh unto the spirit, by focusing on the purpose of your prayer and fasting as well as the spiritual gains.

As a believer, you must develop great love for prayer and fasting. You can plan to live a fasted life as a serious Christian, you can refuse to be a slave to food.

When Satan tempted Jesus to command the stones to be made bread if He is the Son of God, Jesus answered and said, "…*It is written*, **Man shall not live by BREAD alone**, *but by every word that proceedeth out of the mouth of God."* (**Matthew 4:4**).

It is very good to fast. Your fast should always be dedicated to God. It should be planned well. It should be purposeful and with Specific Prayer Targets (SPT). You must expect a positive and a favourable result at the end of your period of fasting. I enjoy spending quality time in prayer and fasting personally as a child of God, and for effective ministry as a Servant of the Most High God.

As we explore the blessings and benefits of biblical prayer and fasting by examining its power and amazing effects in the lives of men and women in the Old Testament, New Testament and in Church history, I pray that the Holy Spirit will minister to your heart and empower you to embark on this powerful spiritual exercise and supernatural journey more purposefully and more meaningfully.

The Bible says,

*"For bodily exercise profiteth little: but **godliness is profitable unto all things**, having **promise of the life** that now is, and of that which is to come."*

1 Timothy 4:8

*"For physical training is of some value, **but godliness (SPIRITUAL TRAINING) is of value in everything and in every way,** since it holds promise for the present life and for the life to come."*

1 Timothy 4:8 (AMP)

*"Physical exercise has some value, but **SPIRITUAL EXERCISE is VALUABLE in EVERY WAY**, because it promises life both for the present and for the future."*

1 Timothy 4:8 (GNT)

*"Physical training is good, but **training for godliness is much better, PROMISING BENEFITS in this life** and in the life to come."*

1 Timothy 4:8 (NLT)

*"…Workouts in the gymnasium are useful, but **A DISCIPLINED LIFE IN GOD IS FAR MORE SO**, making you fit both today and forever."*

1 Timothy 4:8 (MSG)

You will also enjoy these blessings and benefits. Your life will never be the same again. Be blessed, be anointed and be empowered in the precious name of Jesus Christ of Nazareth, Amen!

Christian Damanka
London, United Kingdom.

1

What is Prayer?

*"**Let us** therefore **come boldly** unto **the Throne of Grace**, that we may obtain mercy, and **find grace** to **help** in **time of need**."*

Hebrews 4:16

*"Therefore **let us** [with privilege] **Approach the Throne Of Grace** [that is, the throne of God's gracious favour] with confidence and without fear, so that we may receive mercy [for our failures] and find [His amazing] grace to help in time of need [an appropriate blessing, coming just at the right moment]."*

Hebrews 4:16 (AMP)

"So let us come boldly to the Throne of Our Gracious God. There we will receive His mercy, and we will find grace to help us when we need it most."

Hebrews 4:16 (NLT)

Prayer is God's established, approved and acceptable way for the believer to communicate and fellowship with the heavenly Father, the Lord God Almighty.

Prayer is very important in the life of every believer. Prayer connects us to our heavenly Father.

Prayer is our spiritual umbilical cord for heavenly supply and supernatural livelihood on planet earth. Prayer is our umbilical cord for spiritual oxygen and nutrients from heavenly placenta.

Prayer is the bonafide privilege of the child of God to confidently approach the gracious Throne of his or her Father and receive the much needed help and diverse divine provisions required to function effectively in the earth realm in fulfilling heaven's agenda on earth as it is established in heaven.

- Prayer makes our relationship with God deeper, stronger, greater, more powerful, more meaningful and very fulfilling.

- Prayer changes us, it doesn't change God. You need to pray to God out of a passionate love for fellowship with Him.

- Prayer is more than giving God a list of things you want Him to do for you, although, sometimes petitions, personal request and supplications are relevant aspects of prayer.

The Profound Story Behind the Hymn 'What a Friend we Have in Jesus'

Some of our best-loved hymns were actually birthed and written in times of great sadness and sorrow. ***"What a Friend We Have in Jesus"*** is one such song, one of my favourites in prayer.

Despite the pain, many hymn writers were able to find comfort in the arms of Jesus and point others to this source of unshakable joy with their music. Please join me reflect on the story about the tragedy which spurred this Spirit-filled hymn writer to pen these lyrics.

One of the most helpful hymns in popular use which inspires us to approach the Throne of Grace in Prayer is **Joseph Scriven's** hymn on the friendship of Jesus, the Comforter and Burden-Bearer.

Joseph was born on Sept. 10, 1819, in Ireland. His parents had financial means enough to afford a wonderful educational opportunity for their son. He was enrolled in Trinity College in Dublin where he graduated with a bachelor's degree.

In this young man, Ireland had the prospect of a great citizen with high ideals and notable aspirations. He fell in love with a young lady who was eager to spend her life with him. All preparations had been made for the wedding ceremony and the date had been fixed. However, on the day before their wedding, his promised bride accidentally fell from her horse, while crossing a bridge over the River Bann and was drowned in the water below. Joseph stood helplessly watching from the other side. And he was plunged into the deepest sorrow.

From this sad experience came a deep sense of his dependence upon Christ and of the great truth so helpfully expressed in his lines: **What a Friend we have in Jesus, All our sins and grief to bear!**

In an effort to overcome his sorrow, he began to wander. By age 25 his travels had taken him to an area near Port Hope, Canada. He became highly regarded by the people of that area. He tutored some of the local children in their school work. It was there he met a wonderful young lady, Elisa Roche, and again fell in love. They had exciting plans to be married. However, tragedy reared its ugly head once again and she died of pneumonia before they could wed.

He laboured in Port Hope among the impoverished widows and sick people. He often served for no wages and even shared his clothes with those less fortunate than himself.

On an occasion when Joseph Scriven became ill, a friend who was visiting with him discovered a poem near his bed and asked who had written it. Scriven said, "The Lord and I did it between us." Out of the intense sympathy wrought in his heart by this experience, he wrote the hymn as a poem to bring some spiritual comfort to his mother in her own sorrow and sent it to her in Ireland.

On Aug. 10, 1886, Scriven's body was pulled from a body of water near Bewdly, at Port Hope on Lake Ontario. Two monuments have been erected in his honour. Each has the first stanza of his song engraved on it.

How his hymn came to be first published is not known, as he had not intended it for general use. Indeed, for some time after it was printed, its authorship was unknown, being sometimes incorrectly attributed to Dr. Horatius Bonar. After Scriven's death, however, he became recognized as the author of the hymn that has blessed so many thousands of believers.

Here are the Lyrics to this powerful hymn:

"What a Friend We Have in Jesus"

What a friend we have in Jesus, All our sins and griefs to bear! What a privilege to carry **Everything to God in prayer!**

O what peace we often forfeit, O what needless pain we bear, All because we do not carry **Everything to God in prayer.**

Have we trials and temptations? Is there trouble anywhere? We should never be discouraged; **Take it to the Lord in prayer.**

Can we find a friend so faithful Who will all our sorrows share? Jesus knows our every weakness; **Take it to the Lord in prayer.**

Are we weak and heavy laden, Cumbered with a load of care? Precious Saviour, still our refuge; **Take it to the Lord in prayer.**

Do thy friends despise, forsake thee? Take it to the Lord in prayer! In His arms He'll take and shield thee; Thou wilt find a solace there.

Jesus told an interesting parable in Luke 18:9-14 about prayer, from which we can learn some important lessons:

Two Men Went to the Temple to Pray

"Then Jesus told this story to some who had great confidence in their own righteousness and scorned everyone else: "**Two men went to the Temple to pray**. One was a Pharisee, and the other was a despised tax collector. The Pharisee stood by himself and prayed this prayer 'I thank you, God, that I am not like other people—cheaters, sinners, adulterers. I'm certainly not like that tax collector! **I fast twice a week**, and I give you a tenth of my income.'

"But the tax collector stood at a distance and dared not even lift his eyes to heaven as he prayed. Instead, he beat his chest in sorrow, saying, 'O God, be merciful to me, for I am a sinner.' I tell you, this sinner, not the Pharisee, returned home justified before God. For those who exalt themselves will be humbled, and those who humble themselves will be exalted."

Luke 18:9-14 (NLT)

- Prayer involves intentionally spending quality time enjoying fellowship in God's company like with your best friend.

Jesus also told the Parable of the Persistent Widow in Luke 18:1-8, teaching us the importance of not giving up praying when answers seem to delay:

The Persistent Widow

"One day Jesus told His disciples a story to show that **they should always pray and never give up**. "There was a judge in a certain city," he said, "who neither feared God nor cared about people. A widow of that city came to him repeatedly, saying, 'Give me justice in this dispute with my enemy.' The judge ignored her for a while, but *finally he said to himself, 'I don't fear God or care about people, but this woman is driving me crazy. I'm going to see that she gets justice, because she is wearing me out with her constant requests!'"*

Then the Lord said, "Learn a lesson from this unjust judge. Even he rendered a just decision in the end. So don't you think God will surely give justice to his chosen people who cry out to him day and night? Will he keep putting them off? I tell you, he will grant justice to them quickly! But when the Son of Man returns, how many will he find on the earth who have faith?"

Luke 18:1-8 (NLT)

- Prayer involves asking God to help you identify His perfect will and purpose for your life and ministry; talking to the Lord about your marriage-relationship and family; about your friends and about your future.

- Prayer involves saying sorry to God for your sins, unrighteousness, mistakes and shortcomings.

- Prayer involves appreciating, expressing gratitude and saying 'Thank-You' to your

Heavenly Father for all His goodness and mercies.

- Prayer also involves listening to the Lord and not worrying about His silence, but being glad to be with Him just as you would gladly be with your friends and work colleagues.

When I pray, I talk with Jesus Christ. Prayer involves the soul of man reaching out to, and talking to his or her Creator, God, in loving fellowship with all reverence.

2

56 Reasons Why You Must Pray

1. **Prayer is a way of Calling on the Name of the Lord**

   "…At that [same] time men began to call on the name of the Lord [in worship through prayer, praise, and thanksgiving]."

   Genesis 4:26 (AMP)

   God Almighty promises that,

   "It shall also come to pass that **before they call, I will answer; and while they are still speaking, I will hear.**"

   Isaiah 65:24 (AMP)

   "…Abram called on the name of the Lord."

   Genesis 13:4

2. **Prayer is a way of Approaching God's Throne of Grace**

   "***Therefore let us** [with privilege] **approach the throne of grace** [that is, the throne of God's gracious favour] with confidence and without fear, so that we may receive mercy [for our failures] and find [His amazing] grace to help in time of need [an appropriate blessing, coming just at the right moment].*"

   Hebrews 4:16 (AMP)

3. **Prayer is a way of Receiving Mercy, Grace and Help from God**

   "*Let us therefore come boldly unto the throne of grace, **that we may obtain mercy, and find grace to help in time of need.***"

   Hebrews 4:16

   "*…let us…approach the throne of grace…**so that we may receive mercy** [for our failures] and **find [His amazing] grace to help in time of need**…*"

   Hebrews 4:16 (AMP)

4. **Prayer is a way of Asking for Things from God According to His Will**

   "*This is the [remarkable degree of] confidence which we [as believers are entitled to] have before Him: that if we ask anything according to His will, [that is, consistent with His plan and purpose] He hears us."

1 John 5:14 (AMP)

"And if we know [for a fact, as indeed we do] that He hears and listens to us in whatever we ask, we [also] know [with settled and absolute knowledge] that we have [granted to us] the requests which we have asked from Him."

1 John 5:15 (AMP)

Jesus said,

"For this reason I am telling you, **whatever things you ask for in prayer** [in accordance with God's will], **believe** [with confident trust] that **you have received them, and they will be given to you.**"

Mark 11:24 (AMP)

5. Prayer is a way of Calling and Receiving Answers from God

"And it shall come to pass, that **before they call, I will answer**; and **while they are yet speaking, I will hear.**"

Isaiah 65:24

"When you pray, He will answer you, and you will keep the vows you made."

Job 22:27 (GNT)

David's Prayer to God:

"**Answer me when I call, O God** of my righteousness! You have freed me when I was hemmed in and relieved me when I was in distress; Be gracious to me and **hear [and respond to] my prayer.**"

Psalm 4:1 (AMP)

"**Hear me when I call, O God** of my righteousness: thou hast enlarged me when I was in distress; have mercy upon me, and hear my prayer."

Psalm 4:1

"**Answer me when I call to You**, O God who declares me innocent. Free me from my troubles. Have mercy on me and **hear my prayer.**"

Psalm 4:1 (NLT)

6. Prayer is a way of Talking to God about our Needs

"**I will answer them** before they even **call to Me**. While they are still **talking about their needs**, **I will** go ahead and **answer their prayers!**"

Isaiah 65:24 (NLT)

"Don't worry about anything; instead, **pray about everything. Tell God what you need**, and thank Him for all He has done. Then you will experience God's peace,

which exceeds anything we can understand. His peace will guard your hearts and minds as you live in Christ Jesus."
Philippians 4:6-7 (NLT)

While teaching on Prayer, Jesus said;

"...**when you pray**, *do not use meaningless repetition as the Gentiles do, for they think they will be heard because of their many words. So do not be like them [praying as they do]; for* **your Father knows what you need before you ask Him**.
Matthew 6:7-8 (AMP)

*"***When you pray,** *don't babble on and on as the Gentiles do. They think their prayers are answered merely by repeating their words again and again. Don't be like them, for* **your Father knows exactly what you need even before you ask Him**"
Matthew 6:7-8 (NLT)

7. Prayer is a way of Calling Upon God to Deliver You from Trouble

The Lord says,

"...***call upon Me in the day of trouble***: *I will deliver thee, and thou shalt glorify Me.*
Psalm 50:15

"Then shall ye **call upon Me**, and ye shall go and **pray unto Me**, and **I will hearken unto you.**"

Jeremiah 29:12

David said,

"I have called upon You, for You, O God, will answer me..."

Psalm 17:6 (AMP)

8. Prayer Ushers Us into the Presence of God to Seek the Will of God

"And how bold and free we then become in **His presence, freely asking according to His will**, sure that He's listening."

1 John 5:14 (MSG)

9. Prayer is a way of Seeking the LORD, Seeking His Face and His Strength

"**Seek** the **Lord** and **His strength;** Seek His face continually [longing to be in His presence]."

1 Chronicles 16:11 (AMP)

God says,

"**If My people**, which are called by My name, shall **humble themselves,** and PRAY, and SEEK MY FACE, and turn from their wicked ways; **then will I hear from heaven, and will forgive their sin, and will heal their land.**"

2 Chronicles 7:14

10. **Prayer is a way to Make Our Voice Heard by God for Divine Intervention**

"Thou shalt **make thy prayer unto Him, and He shall hear thee**, and thou shalt pay thy vows."

Job 22:27

"Say to them, 'As I live,' says the Lord, 'just as you have spoken in My hearing, so I will do to you"

Numbers 14:28 (NKJV)

"Thou shalt **make thy prayer unto Him, and He shall hear thee**, and thou shalt pay thy vows."

Job 22:27

"You will **make your prayer to Him, He will hear you**, And you will pay your vows."

Job 22:27 (NKJV)

"You will **pray to Him, and He will hear you**, And you will pay your vows."

Job 22:27 (AMP)

"You will **pray to Him**, and **He will hear you**, and you will fulfill your vows to Him."

Job 22:27 (NLT)

11. Prayer is a way of Making Requests to God in Heaven

"**So listen to the requests** of Your servant and Your people Israel **when they pray** toward this place. Hear from Your dwelling place, from heaven; and when You hear, forgive."

2 Chronicles 6:21 (AMP)

"Be careful for nothing; but in **everything by prayer** and supplication with thanksgiving **let your requests be made known unto God…**"

Philippians 4:6-7

12. Prayer is a way to Receive Anything we Believe God for

Jesus said,

"I tell you, **you can pray for anything**, and if you believe that you've received it, it will be yours."

Mark 11:24 (NLT)

13. Prayer Provides Solution to every form of Suffering

*"Is **anyone** among you **suffering? He must pray**..."*

James 5:13 (AMP)

CASE STUDY 1:
Apostle Paul Prayed About His Sufferings

'A Thorn in the Flesh'

"But to keep me from being puffed up with pride because of the many wonderful things I saw, *I was given* **a painful physical ailment, which acts as Satan's messenger to beat me** *and keep me from being proud.* **Three times I prayed to the Lord about this and asked Him to take it away.** But His answer was: "My grace is all you need, for My power is greatest when you are weak." I am most happy, then, to be proud of my weaknesses, in order to feel the protection of Christ's power over me. I am content with weaknesses, insults, hardships, persecutions, and difficulties for Christ's sake. For when I am weak, then I am strong."

2 Corinthians 12:7-10 (GNT)

14. **Prayer is a way to Seek and Receive God's Protection from Evil, Hurt & Harm**

    During His earthly ministry more than 2 thousand years ago, Jesus Christ prayed to the heavenly Father for divine protection for His disciples and for us,

    "I do not **ask** You to take them out of the world, **but that You keep them and protect them from the evil one.**"

    John 17:15 (AMP)

15. **Prayer is a way to Receive the Desires of Our Heart from God**

    Jesus said,

    "Therefore I say unto you, **What things soever ye desire, when ye pray**, believe that ye receive them, **and ye shall have them.**"

    Mark 11:24

16. **Prayer is the Most Effective way of Overcoming and Dealing with Enemies, Haters and Persecutors**

    Jesus said,

    "But I say unto you, Love your **enemies**, bless **them that curse you**, do good to **them that hate you**, and **pray for them which despitefully use you, and persecute you.**"

    Matthew 5:44

17. Prayer is a way to Overcome Temptations

Jesus said,

"Watch and PRAY, that ye ENTER NOT **into temptation...**"

Matthew 26:41

"Keep watch and **pray, so that you will not give in to temptation...**"

Matthew 26:41 (NLT)

18. God is Pleased with, and Delighted by the Prayer of the Upright

"**The Lord is pleased when good people pray**, but hates the sacrifices that the wicked bring Him."

Proverbs 15:8 (GNT)

"The sacrifice of the wicked is hateful and exceedingly offensive to the Lord, But **the prayer of the upright is His delight!**"

Proverbs 15:8 (AMP)

"God can't stand pious poses, but **He delights in genuine prayers.**"

Proverbs 15:8 (MSG)

"The sacrifice of the wicked is an abomination to the Lord: but **the prayer of the upright is His delight.**"

Proverbs 15:8

"The Lord detests the sacrifice of the wicked, but **He delights in the prayers of the upright."**

Proverbs 15:8 (NLT)

19. God Listens to, and Regards the Prayers of the Destitute

"He will **listen to the prayers of the destitute**. He will not reject their pleas."

Psalm 102:17 (NLT)

"He has regarded the **prayer of the destitute**, And has not despised their prayer."

Psalm 102:17 (AMP)

"**He will regard the prayer of the destitute,** and not despise their prayer."

Psalm 102:17

20. God Hears the Prayer of the Righteous, but He is Far from the Ungodly

"The Lord is far from the wicked: but **He heareth the prayer of the righteous."**

Proverbs 15:29

"The Lord is far from the wicked [and distances Himself from them], But **He hears the prayer of the** [consistently] righteous [that is, those with spiritual integrity and moral courage]."

Proverbs 15:29 (AMP)

21. Prayer is a way to Receive Good Gifts, Good Things and Advantageous Things from Our Heavenly Father

Jesus said,

"If ye then, being evil, know how to give **GOOD GIFTS** unto your children, **how much more shall your Father which is in heaven give GOOD THINGS to them that ask Him?**"

Matthew 7:11

"As bad as you are, you know how to give **GOOD THINGS** to your children. **How much more, then, will your FATHER in HEAVEN give GOOD THINGS to those who ask Him!**"

Matthew 7:11 (GNT)

"If you then, evil (sinful by nature) as you are, know how to give **GOOD and ADVANTAGEOUS GIFTS** to your children, how much more will your **Father Who is in heaven** [perfect as He is] **give what is GOOD and ADVANTAGEOUS to those who keep on asking Him.**"

Matthew 7:11 (AMP)

22. A Believer Ought to Always Pray, Never Give Up, Not Faint and Not Lose Heart

*"Now Jesus was telling the disciples a parable to make the point that **AT ALL TIMES they ought to PRAY and NOT GIVE UP and LOSE HEART.**"*

Luke 18:1 (AMP)

*"And He spake a parable unto them to this end, that **MEN OUGHT ALWAYS to PRAY, and NOT to FAINT.**"*

Luke 18:1

*"One day Jesus told His disciples a story to show that **they should ALWAYS PRAY and NEVER GIVE UP.**"*

Luke 18:1 (NLT)

23. A Believer's Prayer Goes Before God as an Incense

*"**Let my prayer be set forth before Thee as incense**; and the lifting up of my hands as the evening sacrifice."*

Psalm 141:2

*"**Let my prayer be counted as incense before You**; The lifting up of my hands as the evening offering."*

Psalm 141:2 (AMP)

24. Prayer is a way of making Petitions and Intercessions for People

*"With **all PRAYER** and **PETITION pray** [with **specific requests**] at all times [on every occasion and in every season] **in the Spirit**, and with this in view, stay alert with all perseverance and **petition** [INTERCEDING in prayer] FOR ALL GOD'S PEOPLE."*

Ephesians 6:18 (AMP)

The Scripture says,

*"First of all, then, I urge that **petitions (specific requests), prayers, INTERCESSIONS (prayers for others) and thanksgivings be offered on behalf of ALL PEOPLE, for kings and all who are in [positions of] high authority...**"*

1 Timothy 2:1-2 (AMP)

Apostle Paul admonished the church in Ephesus by saying,

*"And **pray for me**..."*

Ephesians 6:19 (AMP)

CASE STUDY 2:
Abraham Intercedes for Sodom and Gomorrah

Then the men got up from their meal and looked out toward Sodom. As they left, Abraham went with them to send them on their way.

"Should I hide My plan from Abraham?" the Lord asked. "For Abraham will certainly become a great and mighty nation, and all the nations of the earth will be blessed through him. I have singled him out so that he will direct his sons and their families to keep the way of the Lord by doing what is right and just. Then I will do for Abraham all that I have promised."

So the Lord told Abraham, "I have heard a great outcry from Sodom and Gomorrah, because their sin is so flagrant. I am going down to see if their actions are as wicked as I have heard. If not, I want to know."

The other men turned and headed toward Sodom, but the Lord remained with Abraham. Abraham approached him and said, "Will you sweep away both the righteous and the wicked? Suppose you find fifty righteous people living there in the city—will you still sweep it away and not spare it for their sakes? Surely you wouldn't do such a thing, destroying the righteous along with the wicked. Why, you would be treating the righteous and the wicked exactly the same! Surely you wouldn't do that! Should not the Judge of all the earth do what is right?"

And the Lord replied, "If I find fifty righteous people in Sodom, I will spare the entire city for their sake."

Then Abraham spoke again. "Since I have begun, let me speak further to my Lord, even though I am but dust and ashes. Suppose there are only forty-five righteous people rather than fifty? Will you destroy the whole city for lack of five?"

And the Lord said, "I will not destroy it if I find forty-five righteous people there."

Then Abraham pressed his request further. "Suppose there are only forty?"

And the Lord replied, "I will not destroy it for the sake of the forty."

"Please don't be angry, my Lord," Abraham pleaded. "Let me speak—suppose only thirty righteous people are found?"

And the Lord replied, "I will not destroy it if I find thirty."

Then Abraham said, "Since I have dared to speak to the Lord, let me continue—suppose there are only twenty?"

And the Lord replied, "Then I will not destroy it for the sake of the twenty."

Finally, Abraham said, "Lord, please don't be angry with me if I speak one more time. Suppose only ten are found there?"

And the Lord replied, "Then I will not destroy it for the sake of the ten."

When the Lord had finished his conversation with Abraham, he went on his way, and Abraham returned to his tent."

Genesis 18:16-33 (NLT)

25. **Prayer is a way of Calling Unto the Lord for Answers and Divine Revelation**

"*Thus saith the Lord...;* **Call unto Me, and I will answer thee**, *and* **show thee great** *and* **mighty things**, *which thou* **knowest not**."

Jeremiah 33:2-3

CASE STUDY 3:
Daniel, Shadrach, Meshach and Abednego Prayed to God for the Revelation of King Nebuchadnezzar's Dream

Daniel *then went home and told his companions Hananiah, Mishael, and Azariah what was going on.* **He asked them to pray to the God of heaven for mercy in solving this mystery** *so that the four of them wouldn't be* killed along with the whole company of Babylonian wise men.

That night the answer to the mystery was given to Daniel in a vision. Daniel blessed the God of heaven, saying,

"Blessed be the name of God, forever and ever. He knows all, does all: He changes the seasons and guides history, He raises up kings and also brings them down, he provides both intelligence and discernment, He opens up the depths, tells secrets, sees in the dark—light spills out of him! God of all my ancestors, all thanks! all praise! You made me wise and strong. And now you've shown us what we asked for. You've solved the king's mystery."

Daniel 2:17-23 (MSG)

26. The Believer is Called Upon to be Devoted to Prayer

"Constantly rejoicing in hope [because of our confidence in Christ], steadfast and patient in distress, **devoted to prayer [continually seeking wisdom, guidance, and strength].**"

Romans 12:12 (AMP)

"**Pray** without ceasing."

1 Thessalonians 5:17

"Never stop **praying**."

1 Thessalonians 5:17 (NLT)

*"Be unceasing and persistent in **prayer**"*

1 Thessalonians 5:17 (AMP)

27. Prayer is a way of Drawing Nearer to God by Calling on Him in Truth

"**The Lord is nigh** unto all them that **call upon Him**, to all that **call upon Him in truth**."

Psalm 145:18

"The Lord is near to **all who call on Him**, To all who **call on Him in truth** (without guile)."

Psalm 145:18 (AMP)

28. Prayer is a way of Connecting with the Heavenly Father

Jesus said,

"…when ye **pray**, say, **Our Father** which art **in heaven**…"

Luke 11:2

29. Prayer is a way to ascribe Honour and Worship to God

Jesus said,

"…when ye **pray**, say…**Hallowed be Thy name**…"

Luke 11:2

30. Prayer is a way of Connecting with God's Kingdom Agenda & Purpose

Jesus said,

"…when ye **pray**, say…**Thy kingdom come**…"

Luke 11:2

31. Prayer is a way of Connecting with the Will of God

Jesus said,

"…When you **pray**, say:…**Your Will be done on earth** as it is in heaven."

Luke 11:2 (NKJV)

32. Prayer is a way of Accessing Our Daily Provisions from God

Jesus said,

"…When you **pray**, say:…**Give us day by day our daily bread.**"

Luke 11:2-3 (NKJV)

"Blessed be **the Lord**, Who **daily loads us with benefits…**"

Psalm 68:19 (NKJV)

33. Prayer is a way to Repent and Receive the Forgiveness of Sins from God

Jesus said,

*"**This is how you should pray…forgive us our sins**, as we forgive those who sin against us…"*

Luke 11:2-4 (NLT)

*"**If we confess our sins**, He is faithful and just to **forgive us our sins**, and to **cleanse us** from all unrighteousness."*

1 John 1:9

*"If we [freely] **admit** that **we have sinned** and **confess our sins, He** is faithful and just [true to His own nature and promises], and **will forgive our sins and cleanse us** continually from all unrighteousness [our wrongdoing, everything not in conformity with His will and purpose]."*

1 John 1:9 (AMP)

CASE STUDY 4:
The Prodigal Son

To illustrate the point further, Jesus told them this story: "A man had two sons. The younger son told his father, 'I want my share of your estate now before you die.' So his father agreed to divide his wealth between his sons.

"A few days later this younger son packed all his belongings and moved to a distant land, and there he wasted all his money in wild living. About the time his money ran out, a great famine swept over the land, and he began to starve. He persuaded a local farmer to hire him, and the man sent him into his fields to feed the pigs. The young man became so hungry that even the pods he was feeding the pigs looked good to him. But no one gave him anything.

"When he finally came to his senses, he said to himself, 'At home even the hired servants have food enough to spare, and here I am dying of hunger! *I will go home to my father and say, "Father, I have sinned against both heaven and you, and I am no longer worthy of being called your son. Please take me on as a hired servant."'*

"So he returned home to his father. And while he was still a long way off, his father saw him coming. Filled with love and compassion, he ran to his son, embraced him, and kissed him. ***His son said to him, 'Father, I have sinned against both heaven and you, and I am no longer worthy of being called your son.'***

"But his father said to the servants, 'Quick! Bring the finest robe in the house and put it on him. Get a ring for his finger and sandals for his feet. And kill the calf we have been fattening. We must celebrate with a feast, for this son of mine was dead and has now returned to life. He was lost, but now he is found.' So the party began.

"Meanwhile, the older son was in the fields working. When he returned home, he heard music and dancing in the house, and he asked one of the servants what was going on. 'Your brother is back,' he was told, 'and your father has killed the fattened calf. We are celebrating because of his safe return.'

"The older brother was angry and wouldn't go in. His father came out and begged him, but he replied, 'All these years I've slaved for you and never once refused to do a single thing you told me to. And in all that time you never gave me even one young goat for a feast with my friends. Yet when this son of yours comes back after squandering your money on prostitutes, you celebrate by killing the fattened calf!'

"His father said to him, 'Look, dear son, you have always stayed by me, and everything I have is yours. We had to celebrate this happy day. For your brother was dead and has come back to life! He was lost, but now he is found!'"

Luke 15:11-32 (NLT)

34. Prayer is a way to Forgive and Release People who Offend us and Sin against us

Jesus said,

"**This is how you should pray**...*forgive us our sins, as we forgive those who sin against us*..."

Luke 11:2-4 (NLT)

Jesus said,

"**If you forgive the sins of any, they are forgiven them**; *if you retain the sins of any, they are retained.*"

John 20:23 (NKJV)

"**If you forgive someone's sins, they're gone for good.** *If you don't forgive sins, what are you going to do with them?*"

John 20:23 (MSG)

"**If you forgive the sins of anyone they are forgiven**...; *if you retain the sins of anyone, they are retained [and remain unforgiven...].*"

John 20:23 (AMP)

"**If you forgive anyone's sins, they are forgiven.** *If you do not forgive them, they are not forgiven.*"

John 20:23 (NLT)

"If you forgive people's sins, they are forgiven; if you do not forgive them, they are not forgiven."

John 20:23 (GNT)

"Whenever you stand **PRAYING, if you have anything against anyone, FORGIVE** him [drop the issue, let it go], so that your Father Who is in heaven will also **forgive you** your transgressions and wrongdoings [against Him and others]."

Mark 11:25 (AMP)

*"But **if you do not forgive**, neither will your Father in heaven forgive your transgressions."*

Mark 11:26 (AMP)

35. **Prayer is a way to Divinely Avoid and Escape Temptation**

Jesus said,

*"…When ye **pray**, say…**lead us not into temptation**…"*

Luke 11:2-4

While on a Prayer Retreat in the Garden of Gethsemane, Jesus advised sleepy Peter, James and John;

*"**Watch** and **PRAY, lest you enter into temptation**. The spirit indeed is willing, but the flesh is weak."*
Matthew 26:41 (NKJV)

*"**Watch and PRAY, lest you enter into temptation**. The spirit indeed is willing, but the flesh is weak."*
Mark 14:38 (NKJV)

*"Stay alert, **BE in PRAYER**, so you **DON'T ENTER the DANGER ZONE** without even knowing it."*
Mark 14:38 (MSG)

*"Keep watch and **PRAY, so that you will not give in to temptation**. For the spirit is willing, but the body is weak."*
Mark 14:38 (NLT)

*"When He arrived at the place [called Gethsemane], He said to them, '**PRAY continually that you may not fall into temptation.**'"*
Luke 22:40 (AMP)

Jesus Christ's Prayer Retreat Message

Jesus "went to the Mount of Olives, as He was accustomed, and His disciples also followed Him. When He came to the place, He said to them, ***"Pray that you may not enter into temptation."***

And He was withdrawn from them about a stone's throw, and He knelt down and prayed, saying, "Father, if it is Your will, take this cup away from Me; nevertheless not My will, but Yours, be done." Then an angel appeared to Him from heaven, strengthening Him. And being in agony, He prayed more earnestly. Then His sweat became like great drops of blood falling down to the ground.

When He rose up from prayer, and had come to His disciples, He found them sleeping from sorrow. Then He said to them, "Why do you sleep? ***Rise and pray, lest you enter into temptation."***

Luke 22:39-46 (NKJV)

36. Prayer is a way of Accessing God's Deliverance from Evil

Jesus said,

"…When ye **pray**, say…*deliver us from evil*…"

Luke 11:2-4

37. The Holy Spirit Prays for the Believer. He Intercedes for Us

*"**The Holy Spirit helps us** in our weakness…**we don't know what God wants us to pray for.** But **the HOLY SPIRIT PRAYS FOR US with groanings that cannot be expressed in words.**"*

Romans 8:26 (NLT)

*"…the moment we get tired…God's Spirit is right alongside helping us along. **If we don't know how or what to pray…HE DOES OUR PRAYING IN AND FOR US, making prayer out of our wordless sighs**…He knows us far better than we know ourselves"*

Romans 8:26-28 (MSG)

*"Likewise **the Spirit also helpeth our infirmities: for we know not what we should pray for as we ought**: but **THE SPIRIT … MAKETH INTERCESSION FOR US** with groanings which cannot be uttered."*

Romans 8:26

38. Prayer is a way of Making Supplication, Thanksgiving, Requests to God

*"Be careful for nothing; but **in everything by prayer and supplication** with **thanksgiving let your requests be made known unto God.** And the peace of God, which*

passeth all understanding, shall keep your hearts and minds through Christ Jesus."

Philippians 4:6-7

"With all **prayer** and **petition** pray [with specific **requests**] at all times [on every occasion and in every season] in the Spirit, and with this in view, stay alert with all perseverance and **petition** [interceding in prayer] for all God's people."

Ephesians 6:18 (AMP)

39. Prayer is a way of Channeling Our Anxieties, Worries, Circumstances and Situations to God

"Do not be **ANXIOUS** or **WORRIED** about **ANYTHING**, but **in everything [every circumstance and situation] by prayer** and **petition** with **thanksgiving**, continue to **make your [specific] requests known to God**. And the peace of God [that peace which reassures the heart, that peace] which transcends all understanding, [that peace which] stands guard over your hearts and your minds in Christ Jesus [is yours]."

Philippians 4:6-7 (AMP)

40. Prayer is a way to Experience the Perfect PEACE of God

"Be careful for nothing; but in **everything by prayer** and supplication with thanksgiving **let your requests**

be made known unto God. And the **PEACE OF GOD, which passeth all understanding, SHALL KEEP YOUR HEARTS AND MINDS through Christ Jesus.**"
Philippians 4:6-7

"Do not be anxious or worried about anything, but **in everything** [every circumstance and situation] **by prayer** and petition with thanksgiving, **continue to make your** [specific] **requests known to God.** And the **PEACE OF GOD** [that peace which reassures the heart, that peace] which transcends all understanding, [that peace which] **STANDS GUARD OVER YOUR HEARTS and YOUR MINDS in Christ Jesus** [is yours]."
Philippians 4:6-7 (AMP)

"**Don't worry about anything;** instead, **pray about everything. Tell God what you need**, and thank Him for all He has done. **Then you will EXPERIENCE GOD'S PEACE, which exceeds anything we can understand. His peace will guard your hearts and minds as you live in Christ Jesus.**"
Philippians 4:6-7 (NLT)

41. Believers are to be Devoted to Prayer, Persistent in Prayer, Continue in Prayer and to Pray Diligently.

The Bible says,

*"**Devote yourselves to prayer** with an alert mind and a thankful heart."*

Colossians 4:2 (NLT)

*"**Continue in prayer**, and watch in the same with thanksgiving."*

Colossians 4:2

*"**Be persistent and devoted to prayer**, being alert and **focused in your prayer life** with an attitude of thanksgiving."*

Colossians 4:2 (AMP)

*"**Pray diligently**. Stay alert, with your eyes wide open in gratitude..."*

Colossians 4:2-4 (MSG)

42. Prayer makes God OPEN DOORS of OPPORTUNITIES for Us, for the Spread of the Gospel and for Ministry Exploits

The Great Apostle Paul says,

*"**Pray for us, too, that God will give us many opportunities to speak about His mysterious plan***

concerning Christ...Pray that I will proclaim this message as clearly as I should."

Colossians 4:3-4 (NLT)

"...praying also for us, that God would open unto us a door of utterance, to speak the mystery of Christ...*That I may make it manifest, as I ought to speak."*

Colossians 4:3-4

"...pray for us, too, that God will open a door [of opportunity] to us for the word, to proclaim the mystery of Christ...that I may make it clear [and speak boldly and unfold the mystery] in the way I should"

Colossians 4:3-4 (AMP)

"...Don't forget **to pray for us, that God will open doors for telling the mystery of Christ... Pray** that every time I open my mouth I'll be able to make Christ plain as day to them."

Colossians 4:3-4 (MSG)

Talking about the Lord Jesus, the Bible says,

"...These things saith He that is holy, He that is true, He that hath **the key of David, He that openeth, and no man shutteth; and shutteth, and no man openeth; ...behold, I have set before thee an open door, and no man can shut it...**"

Revelation 3:7-8

"...These are the words of the Holy One, the True One, He Who has **the key...of David, He Who opens and no one will [be able to] shut, and He who shuts and no one opens:...See, I have set before you an open door which no one is able to shut...**"

Revelation 3:7-8 (AMP)

"These things says He Who is holy, He Who is true, "He Who **has the key of David, He who opens and no one shuts, and shuts and no one opens"...See, I have set before you an open door, and no one can shut it...**"

Revelation 3:7-8 (NKJV)

"...This is the message from the One Who is holy and true, the One Who **has the key of David. What He opens, no one can close; and what He closes, no one can open:...I have opened a door for you that no one can close...**"

Revelation 3:7-8 (NLT)

43. Prayer is a way to Access the WISDOM of GOD

"*If any of you lacks <u>wisdom</u> [to guide him through a decision or circumstance], he is to ask of [our benevolent] God, Who gives to everyone generously* and without rebuke or blame, and it will be given to him."

James 1:5 (AMP)

*"**If any of you lack wisdom, let him ask of God**, that giveth to all men liberally, and upbraideth not; and it shall be given him."*

James 1:5

*"**If you need wisdom, ask our generous God**, and **He will give it to you**. He will not rebuke you for asking."*

James 1:5 (NLT)

CASE STUDY 5:
Solomon Asks God for Wisdom

"And Solomon loved the Lord, walking in the statutes of his father David, except that he sacrificed and burned incense at the high places.

Now the king went to Gibeon to sacrifice there, for that was the great high place: Solomon offered a thousand burnt offerings on that altar. ***At Gibeon the Lord appeared to Solomon in a dream by night; and God said, "Ask! What shall I give you?"***

And Solomon said: "You have shown great mercy to Your servant David my father, because he walked before You in truth, in righteousness, and in uprightness of heart with You; You have continued this great kindness for him, and You have given him a son to sit on his throne, as it is this day. Now, O Lord my God, You have made Your servant king instead of my father David, but I am a little child; I do not know how to go out or come in. And Your servant is in the midst of Your people whom You have chosen, a great people, too numerous to be numbered or counted. **Therefore give to Your servant an understanding heart to judge Your people, that I may discern between good and evil. For who is able to judge this great people of Yours?"**

The speech pleased the Lord, that Solomon had asked this thing. Then God said to him: "Because you have asked this thing, and have not asked long life for yourself, nor have asked riches for yourself, nor have asked the life of your enemies, but have asked for yourself understanding to discern justice, behold, I have done according to your words; see, **I HAVE GIVEN YOU A WISE and UNDERSTANDING HEART,** so that there has not been anyone like you before you, nor shall any like you arise after you. And I have also given you what you have not asked: both riches and honour, so that there shall not be anyone like you among the kings all your days. So if you walk in My ways, to keep My statutes and My commandments, as your father David walked, then I will lengthen your days."

1 Kings 3:1-14 (NKJV)

44. Prayer is God's Approved way for Believers to Support and Strengthen One Another Spiritually Unto Healing and Restoration

"...*pray for **each other*** so that you may be **healed**..."
James 5:16 (NLT)

"...*pray for **one another***, that you may be **healed**..."
James 5:16 (NKJV)

"...*pray for **one another***, that you may be **healed and restored**..."
James 5:16 (AMP)

45. The Prayer of a Believer Has Great & Tremendous Power, Produces Wonderful Results, Accomplishes Much, Avails Much

"...*The **earnest prayer** of a **righteous person** has great power and produces wonderful results*."
James 5:16 (NLT)

"...*The **effective, fervent prayer** of a righteous man **avails much**.*"
James 5:16 (NKJV)

"...*The **heartfelt** and **persistent prayer** of a righteous man (believer) **can accomplish much** [when put into action and made effective by God—it is dynamic and can have tremendous power]."

James 5:16 (AMP)

"...The **prayer of a person living right with God** is something **powerful** to be reckoned with."

James 5:16 (MSG)

46. Prayer is God's Prescription for a Quiet and Peaceable life in Families, Communities, Villages, Towns, Cities, Nations and the World

"I exhort therefore, that, first of all, **supplications, prayers, intercessions**, and **giving of thanks, be made for all men; For kings, and for all that are in authority**; that we may lead a quiet and peaceable life in all godliness and honesty.

1 Timothy 2:1-2

"First of all, then, I urge that **petitions (specific requests), prayers, intercessions (prayers for others) and thanksgivings be offered** on behalf of **all people, for kings and all who are in [positions of] high authority**, so that we may live a peaceful and quiet life in all godliness and dignity."

1 Timothy 2:1-2 (AMP)

"The first thing I want you to do is pray. **Pray every way you know how, for everyone you know. Pray especially for rulers and their governments to rule well** so we can be quietly about our business of living simply, in humble contemplation. **This is the way our Saviour God wants us to live.**"

1 Timothy 2:1-3 (MSG)

"I urge you, first of all, **to pray for all people. Ask God to help them; intercede on their behalf, and give thanks for them. Pray this way for kings and all who are in authority** so that we can live peaceful and quiet lives marked by godliness and dignity."

1 Timothy 2:1-2 (NLT)

47. Prayer for the PEACE of JERUSALEM is a Biblical Requirement for Prosperity

"**Pray** for the **peace of Jerusalem**: they shall prosper that love thee."

Psalm 122:6

"**Pray** for the **peace of Jerusalem:** May they prosper who love you [holy city]."

Psalm 122:6 (AMP)

"**Pray for peace in Jerusalem**. May all who love this city prosper."

Psalm 122:6 (NLT)

*"**Pray for Jerusalem's peace!** Prosperity to all you Jerusalem-lovers!.."*

Psalm 122:6-9 (MSG)

48. Prayer is a way to Make DECREES and DECLARATIONS and Heaven will Establish them

*"**Thou shalt also decree a thing, and it shall be established** unto thee: and the light shall shine upon thy ways."*

Job 22:28

*"**You will also declare a thing, And it will be established for you**; So light will shine on your ways."*

Job 22:28 (NKJV)

*"**You will also decide and decree a thing, and it will be established for you**; And the light [of God's favour] will shine upon your ways."*

Job 22:28 (AMP)

*"You'll pray to Him and He'll listen; He'll help you do what you've promised. **You'll decide what you want and it will happen.**"*

Job 22:26-30 (MSG)

49. Prayer is a way to CONDEMN, CANCEL, SILENCE, NULLIFY, REVOKE & REVERSE manifestations of the Voice of the Enemy (Voice of Judgment, Accusation & Destruction)

God's Promise,

"No weapon that is formed against thee shall prosper; and **every tongue that shall rise against thee in judgment thou shalt condemn**. This is the heritage of the servants of the Lord, and their righteousness is of Me, saith the Lord."

Isaiah 54:17

"No weapon that is formed against you will succeed; And **every tongue that rises against you in judgment you will condemn**. This [peace, righteousness, security, and triumph over opposition] is the heritage of the servants of the Lord, And this is their vindication from Me," says the Lord.

Isaiah 54:17 (AMP)

"…no weapon turned against you will succeed. **You will silence every voice raised up to accuse you.** These benefits are enjoyed by the servants of the Lord; their vindication will come from me. I, the Lord, have spoken!"

Isaiah 54:17 (NLT)

50. Prayer ascends as a Memorial Offering before God

*"Now at Caesarea…there was a man named **Cornelius**, a centurion of what was known as the Italian Regiment, a devout man and one who, along with all his household, feared God. He made many charitable donations to the Jewish people, and **prayed to God always. About the ninth hour (3:00 p.m.) of the day he clearly saw in a vision an angel of God who had come to him and said, "Cornelius!"** Cornelius was frightened and stared intently at him and said, "What is it, lord (sir)?" And **the angel said to him, "YOUR PRAYERS** and **gifts of charity HAVE ASCENDED AS A MEMORIAL OFFERING BEFORE GOD [an offering made in remembrance of His past blessings].***

Acts 10:1-4 (AMP)

51. Prayer is a way to RESIST your adversary, your great enemy, the Devil

The Scriptures say,

*"Be sober, be vigilant; because **your adversary the devil**, as a roaring lion, walketh about, seeking whom he may devour: **Whom resist stedfast in the faith**…"*

1 Peter 5:8-9

"Be sober [well balanced and self-disciplined], **be alert and cautious at all times. That enemy of yours, the devil, prowls around like a roaring lion [fiercely hungry], seeking someone to devour. But resist him, be firm in your faith [against his attack—rooted, established, immovable]...**"

1 Peter 5:8-9 (AMP)

"Stay alert! Watch out for your **great enemy, the devil**. He prowls around like a roaring lion, looking for someone to devour. **Stand firm against him**, and be strong in your faith..."

1 Peter 5:8-9 (NLT)

"Keep a cool head. Stay alert. **The Devil is poised to pounce**, and would like nothing better than to catch you napping. **Keep your guard up.** You're not the only ones plunged into these hard times."

1 Peter 5:8-9 (MSG)

The Bible says,

"Submit yourselves therefore to God. **RESIST the devil**, and **he will flee from you.**"

James 4:7

"So submit to [the authority of] God. **RESIST the devil [stand firm against him]** and **he will flee from you.**"

James 4:7 (AMP)

"So let God work his will in you. Yell a loud no to the Devil and watch him scamper."

James 4:7-10 (MSG)

"So humble yourselves before God. **Resist the devil**, and he will flee from you."

James 4:7 (NLT)

52. Prayer Provides Supernatural Strength and Ability, Enables the Believer to be Ready and Alert to Escape Terrible Events of the Last Days/End Times & Make the Rapture

Jesus said,

"Watch therefore, and **PRAY always that you may be counted worthy** to **escape all these things that will come to pass**, and to **stand before the Son of Man**."

Luke 21:36 (NKJV)

"But **keep alert** at all times [be attentive and ready], **PRAYING that you may have the strength and ability** [to be found worthy and] **to escape all these things that are going to take place**, and **to stand in the presence of the Son of Man** [at His coming]."

Luke 21:36 (AMP)

"**PRAY constantly** that you will have **<u>the strength</u> and <u>wits</u> to make it through** everything that's coming and **end up on your feet before the Son of Man.**"

Luke 21:36 (MSG)

53. Prayer is a way to ASK for ANYTHING in the Name of Jesus

Jesus said,

"You can **ASK for anything** in My name, and **I will do it**, so that the Son can bring glory to the Father."

John 14:13 (NLT)

"Yes, **ASK Me for anything** in my name, and **I will do it!**"

John 14:14 (NLT)

"...**whatsoever** ye shall ASK of the **Father in my name**, He may **give it you.**"

John 15:16

54. Prayer is a way to Position Ourselves for Heavenly Rewards on Earth

Discover this secret in Jesus' teaching on Prayer,

"But when you **PRAY**, go into your most private room, close the door and **pray to your Father Who is in secret**, and **your Father Who sees [what is done] in secret will reward you.**"

Matthew 6:6 (AMP)

"But when you **PRAY**, go away by yourself, shut the door behind you, and **pray to your Father in private**. Then **your Father, who sees everything, will reward you**."

Matthew 6:6 (NLT)

55. Prayer is a way to Build up Ourselves Spiritually

"But ye, beloved, **BUILDING up yourselves** on your most holy faith, **PRAYING in the Holy Ghost**."

Jude 1:20

"But you, beloved, **BUILD yourselves up** on [the foundation of] your most holy faith [continually progress, rise like an edifice higher and higher], **PRAY in the Holy Spirit**"

Jude 1:20 (AMP)

"But you, my friends, **keep on BUILDING yourselves up** on your most sacred faith. **PRAY in the power of the Holy Spirit**."

Jude 1:20 (GNT)

"But you, dear friends, carefully **BUILD yourselves up** in this most holy faith by **PRAYING in the Holy Spirit**."

Jude 1:20 (MSG)

"But you, dear friends, must **build each other up** in your most holy faith, **PRAY in the power of the Holy Spirit.**"

Jude 1:20 (NLT)

56. Prayer Attracts ANGELIC VISITATION from Heaven

i. JESUS Experienced Angelic Visitation through Prayer

Jesus "…kneeled down, and PRAYED, Saying, Father, if thou be willing, remove this cup from me: nevertheless not my will, but thine, be done.

And there appeared an ANGEL unto Him from heaven, strengthening Him.

And being in an agony **He prayed more earnestly:** and His sweat was as it were great drops of blood falling down to the ground. And…He rose up from prayer…"

Luke 22:41-45

Jesus "…knelt down and prayed, "Father, if you are willing, please take this cup of suffering away from me. Yet I want your will to be done, not mine." **Then an angel from heaven appeared and strengthened Him. He prayed more fervently,** and he was in such agony of spirit that his sweat fell to the ground like great drops of blood."

Luke 22:41-44 (NLT)

ii. Peter Experienced Angelic Visitation as the church Prayed for Him

"...**Herod the king** stretched forth his hands...to take **Peter** also...and...**put him in prison**...**Peter** therefore **was kept in prison:** *but PRAYER WAS MADE without ceasing of the church UNTO GOD FOR HIM.*

And when Herod would have brought him forth, the same night Peter was sleeping between two soldiers, bound with two chains: and the keepers before the door kept the prison.

And, behold, **THE ANGEL OF THE LORD CAME UPON HIM**, and a light shined **in the prison**: and he smote Peter on the side, and raised him up, saying, Arise up quickly. And his chains fell off from his hands.

And **THE ANGEL said unto him**, Gird thyself, and bind on thy sandals. And so he did. And he saith unto him, Cast thy garment about thee, and follow me.

And he went out, and followed him; and wist not that it was true **WHICH WAS DONE BY THE ANGEL**; but thought he saw a vision.

When they were past the first and the second ward, they came unto the iron gate that leadeth unto the city; which opened to them of his own accord: and they went out, and passed on through one street; and forthwith the angel departed from him.

And when Peter was come to himself, he said, Now I know of a surety, that the Lord hath sent his angel, and hath delivered me…

And when he had considered the thing, he came to the house of Mary the mother of John, whose surname was Mark; **where many were gathered together PRAYING.**

Acts 12:1-19

3

4 Main Aspects of Biblical Prayer

This is one of the basics of prayer which I learned very early in my Christian life from the age of 13 in the boarding school through my fellowship with Scripture Union.

Biblical Prayer Should Basically Include 4 Areas, dubbed 'ACTS':

- A - Adoration
- C - Confession
- T - Thanksgiving
- S - Supplication

1. ADORATION *(Praise and Worship God Wholeheartedly)*

"O come, **let us worship** and **bow down**: let us kneel before the Lord our Maker."

Psalm 95:6

"O come, let us **worship** and **bow down, Let us kneel before the Lord our Maker** [in reverent **praise** and **prayer**]."

Psalm 95:6 (AMP)

Jesus said,

"But the hour cometh, and now is, when the **true worshippers** shall **worship the Father in spirit and in truth**: for the Father seeketh such to **worship Him**.

John 4:23

"**God is a Spirit**: and they that **worship Him** must **worship Him in spirit** and **in truth**."

John 4:24

2. CONFESSION *(Repent of Every Known Sin and Confess Them to God)*

'No Sin?'

"If we say that we have No sin, we deceive ourselves, and the truth is not in us."

1 John 1:8

'Not Sinned?'

"If we say that we have Not sinned, we make Him a liar, and His word is not in us."

1 John 1:10

"If we say that we have Not sinned [refusing to admit acts of sin], we make Him [out to be] a liar [by contradicting Him] and His word is not in us."

1 John 1:10 (AMP)

'If We Repent and Confess Our Sins, God Will Forgive Us'

"If we confess our sins, He is faithful and just to forgive us our sins, and to cleanse us from all unrighteousness."

1 John 1:9

"If we [freely] admit that we have sinned and confess our sins, He is faithful and just [true to His own nature and promises], and will forgive our sins and cleanse us continually from all unrighteousness [our wrongdoing, everything not in conformity with His will and purpose]."

1 John 1:9 (AMP)

"**I acknowledge my sin unto Thee**, and **mine iniquity have I not hid**. I said, **I will confess my transgressions** unto **the Lord**; and thou forgavest the iniquity of my sin."

Psalm 32:5

"Finally, **I confessed all my sins to You** and stopped trying to hide my guilt. I said to myself, "**I will confess my rebellion to the Lord.**" And You forgave me! All my guilt is gone."

Psalm 32:5 (NLT)

"I acknowledged my sin to You, And I did not hide my wickedness; I said, **"I will confess [all] my transgressions to the Lord"**; And You forgave the guilt of my sin."

Psalm 32:5 (AMP)

"Then I let it all out; I said, "I'll make a clean breast of my failures to God." Suddenly the pressure was gone— my guilt dissolved, my sin disappeared."

Psalm 32:5 (MSG)

3. THANKSGIVING *(Give Thanks to God Almighty for His Goodness)*

"Be careful for nothing; **but in everything by PRAYER** and **supplication with THANKSGIVING** let your requests be made known unto God."

Philippians 4:6

"Do not be anxious or worried about anything, but **in everything [every circumstance and situation] by PRAYER and petition with THANKSGIVING,** continue to make your [specific] requests known to God."

Philippians 4:6 (AMP)

"Don't worry about anything; instead, **PRAY about everything**. Tell God what you need, and **THANK Him for all He has done**."

Philippians 4:6 (NLT)

"Don't fret or worry. Instead of worrying, **pray**. Let **petitions and PRAISES shape your worries into PRAYERS, letting God know your concerns**. Before you know it, a sense of God's wholeness, everything coming together for good, will come and settle you down. It's wonderful what happens when Christ displaces worry at the center of your life."

Philippians 4:6-7 (MSG)

"**Pray** without ceasing. **In everything GIVE THANKS**: for this is the will of God in Christ Jesus concerning you."

1 Thessalonians 5:17-18 (KJV)

"Never stop **praying**. **BE THANKFUL** in all circumstances, for this is God's will for you who belong to Christ Jesus."

1 Thessalonians 5:17-18 (NLT)

"**Pray** all the time; **THANK God** no matter what happens. This is the way God wants you who belong to Christ Jesus to live."

1 Thessalonians 5:16-18 (MSG)

"Be unceasing and persistent **in PRAYER**; in every situation [no matter what the circumstances] **be THANKFUL** and **continually GIVE THANKS to God**; for this is the will of God for you in Christ Jesus."

1 Thessalonians 5:17-18 (AMP)

"**Then JESUS took the loaves, GAVE THANKS to God**, and distributed them to the people. Afterward He did the same with the fish. And they all ate as much as they wanted."

John 6:11 (NLT)

PowerPoint

Miracles always follow a thankful heart.

4. SUPPLICATION *(Intercession /Requests /Petition / Desires Directed to God the Father)*

*"First of all, then, I urge that **petitions** (specific **requests**), **prayers, intercessions (prayers for others)** and thanksgivings **be offered on behalf of all people.**"*
1 Timothy 2:1 (AMP)

*"I exhort therefore, that, first of all, **supplications, prayers, intercessions**, and giving of thanks, **be made for all men.**"*
1 Timothy 2:1

*"I urge you, first of all, to **pray for all people. Ask God to help them; intercede on their behalf**, and give thanks for them."*
1 Timothy 2:1 (NLT)

CASE STUDY 6:
Peter was arrested and imprisoned, the church interceded for him, God intervened.

*"**Peter** therefore was kept **in prison**: but **prayer was made** without ceasing **of the church unto God** for him."*
Acts 12:5

"All the time that **Peter** was under heavy guard **in the jailhouse**, the **church prayed for him most strenuously.**"

Acts 12:5 (MSG)

"But while **Peter was in prison**, the **church prayed** very earnestly **for him.**"

Acts 12:5 (NLT)

"So **Peter was kept in prison**, but **fervent and persistent prayer for him** was being **made to God by the church.**"

Acts 12:5 (AMP)

4

When To Pray

1. Pray in the Morning

God commanded Moses saying,

"You shall **make an ALTAR** upon which **to BURN INCENSE**...Aaron shall burn sweet and fragrant incense on it; he shall **burn it EVERY MORNING** when he trims and tends the **lamps**. When Aaron sets up the lamps **at twilight**, he shall burn incense, **a perpetual incense before the Lord**..."

Exodus 30:1, 7-8 (AMP)

PowerPoint

Every Christian is called into the office of a Priest unto God after the order of Melchizedek.

"For He testifies: **You are a priest forever** According to the order of **Melchizedek**."

Hebrews 7:17 (NKJV)

This is called the *Priesthood of all believers*, it is irrespective of your gender, age or theological education. Every born again believer is a Priest unto the Lord, and you are required to maintain the altar and spend quality time before the Lord each morning before anything else. It is a way of seeking God first and putting Him first (Matthew 6:33).

"**My voice** shall Thou hear **in the morning**, O Lord; **in the morning will I direct my prayer unto Thee**, and will look up"

Psalm 5:3

Jesus Prayed in the Mornings:
"Before daybreak **the next morning, Jesus got up** and went out to an isolated place **to pray**."

Mark 1:35 (NLT)

"And **in the morning**, rising up a great while before day, He went out, and departed into a solitary place, **and** there **prayed**."

Mark 1:35

"**Early in the morning**, while it was still dark, **Jesus got up**, left [the house], and went out to a secluded place, **and was praying** there."

Mark 1:35 (AMP)

"Since your days began, **have you ever commanded the morning**, And caused the dawn to know its place, **So that light may take hold of the corners of the earth** And shake the wickedness out of it?"

Job 38:12-13 (AMP)

"Hast thou **commanded the morning** since thy days; and caused the dayspring to know his place; That it might take hold of the ends of the earth, that the wicked might be shaken out of it?"

Job 38:12-13

2. Pray at Noon and in the Evening

"**Evening**, and **morning**, and at **noon**, will **I pray**, and cry aloud: and He shall hear my voice"

Psalm 55:17

"***I call to God***; God will help me. ***At dusk, dawn***, and ***noon*** I sigh deep sighs—***He hears, He rescues***. My life is well and whole, secure in the middle of danger Even while thousands are lined up against me. God hears it all, and from his judge's bench puts them in their place..."

Psalm 55:16-19 (MSG)

3. Pray Day and Night

"O Lord God…I have cried **day and night** before Thee"

Psalm 88:1

Daniel prayed 3 times a day:

"…***Daniel***…continued to ***pray just as he had always done***…***Three times a day*** he knelt there in prayer, thanking and praising his God."

Daniel 6:10 (MSG)

"…***Daniel***…continued to get down on his knees three ***times a day, praying*** and giving thanks before his God, as he had been doing previously."

Daniel 6:10 (AMP)

4. Pray Daily or Everyday

"Be merciful unto me, O Lord: for ***I cry unto Thee daily***"

Psalm 86:3

"Be gracious and merciful to me, **O Lord, For to You I cry out all the day long**."

Psalm 86:3 (AMP)

"Be merciful to me, **O Lord**, for **I am calling on You constantly**."

Psalm 86:3 (NLT)

5. Pray Always, On All Occasions

Jesus said,

"Men ought **ALWAYS to PRAY**, and not faint"

Luke 18:1

"One day Jesus told His disciples a story to show that they **should ALWAYS PRAY** and never give up."

Luke 18:1 (NLT)

"Now Jesus was telling the disciples a parable to make the point that **AT ALL TIMES THEY OUGHT to PRAY** and not give up and lose heart."

Luke 18:1 (AMP)

"Jesus told them a story showing that it was necessary for them to **PRAY CONSISTENTLY** and never quit..."

Luke 18:1-3 (MSG)

"**PRAYING ALWAYS** with all prayer and supplication in the Spirit…"

Ephesians 6:18

"With all prayer and petition **PRAY** [with specific requests] **AT ALL TIMES** [**on every occasion and in every season**] in the Spirit…"

Ephesians 6:18 (AMP)

"**PRAY** in the Spirit **AT ALL TIMES** and **on every occasion**. Stay alert and be **persistent in your prayers** for all believers everywhere."

Ephesians 6:18 (NLT)

"…**PRAY ON EVERY OCCASION**, as the Spirit leads. For this reason keep alert and never give up; **PRAY ALWAYS** for all God's people."

Ephesians 6:18 (GNT)

"Pray without ceasing."

1 Thessalonians 5:17

"Pray all the time"

1 Thessalonians 5:17 (MSG)

"Be **unceasing and persistent in prayer**."

1 Thessalonians 5:17 (AMP)

5

How To Pray

I learnt how to pray from my beloved grandmother Monica, when I was a child of about 8years old. Every night when we retire to bed, grandma keeps her bedroom door open and she often starts off her 'holy conversation' by saying, "O Yehowah Mawu Ga" (meaning – O Thou Great Jehovah). Most of the time, it's as though she is communicating with someone who is right there with her. That is what prayer is. It involves talking to God our Father on a one-to-one basis.

It is very important for every believer to learn, understand and know how to pray biblical prayers. The problem many people have, and the problem in the church today is not one of lack of prayer or prayerlessness, but a problem of praying amiss.

The Bible says,

"**Ye ask,** and **receive not**, because **ye ask amiss** that ye may consume it upon your lusts."

James 4:3

"**You ask [God for something]** and **do not receive it, because you ask with wrong motives** [out of selfishness or with an unrighteous agenda], so that [when you get what you want] you may spend it on your [hedonistic] desires."

James 4:3 (AMP)

"And even **when you ask, you don't get it because your motives are all wrong**—you want only what will give you pleasure."

James 4:3 (NLT)

"And when **you ask, you do not receive it, because your motives are bad**; you ask for things to use for your own pleasures."

James 4:3

The above Scriptures explain some of the reasons why you need to discover from the Bible how to offer biblical prayers to God and receive answers, solutions, healing, breakthroughs and miracles from God.

1. Pray to God - the Heavenly Father

According to the teachings of the Bible, Prayer must always be directed to God the Father, the first Person of the Trinity. Biblical Prayer must not be directed to any human being, an angel, the Virgin Mary - blessed Mother of Jesus Christ, or to any object whatsoever. God Almighty alone must be the object and central focus of our prayer.

a. Jesus taught us to Pray to the Heavenly Father

Jesus Christ Himself taught this biblical principle and practiced it as well.

"Now it came to pass, as He was praying in a certain place, when He ceased, that one of His disciples said to Him, **"Lord, teach us to pray***, as John also taught his disciples." So He said to them,* **"When you pray, say: Our Father in heaven***, Hallowed be Your name. Your kingdom come. Your will be done On earth as it is in heaven. Give us day by day our daily bread. And forgive us our sins, For we also forgive everyone who is indebted to us. And do not lead us into temptation, But deliver us from the evil one."*

Luke 11:1-4 (NKJV)

"...whatsoever ye shall **ASK** *of* **the FATHER** *in my name, He may give it you."*

John 15:16

"...whatever you **ask the Father**...*He gives you.*

John 15:16 (MSG)

"...*the Father will give you whatever you ask for, using my name.*"

John 15:16 (NLT)

"...*Verily, verily, I say unto you, Whatsoever ye shall **ask the Father in my name**, He will give it you.*"

John 16:23

"*Again I say to you that if two of you agree on earth concerning anything that they ask, **it will be done for them by My Father in heaven**.*"

Matthew 18:19 (NKJV)

"*And when ye stand **praying**, forgive, if ye have ought against any: **that your Father also which is in heaven** may forgive you your trespasses.*

*But if ye do not forgive, neither will **your Father which is in heaven** forgive your trespasses.*"

Mark 11:25-26

Jesus emphatically assures us that we will receive answers when we pray to the Heavenly Father. He said,

"What father among you, if his son asks for a fish, will give him a snake instead of a fish? Or if he asks for an egg, will give him a scorpion? If you, then, being evil [that is, sinful by nature], know how to give good gifts to your children, **how much more will** *your heavenly Father give the Holy Spirit to those who ask and continue to ask Him!"*

Luke 11:11-13 (AMP)

b. Jesus Himself Prayed to the Heavenly Father

During His earthly ministry more than two thousand years ago, Jesus Himself directed His prayers to the Heavenly Father as we discover below:

i. Jesus Prayed to the Heavenly Father During His Personal Quiet Times

*"And it came to pass in those days, that **He went out** into a mountain **to pray**, and continued all night **in prayer to God**."*

Luke 6:12

*"Now at this time **Jesus went off to the mountain to pray**, and He spent the whole night **in prayer to God**."*

Luke 6:12 (AMP)

*"One day soon afterward **Jesus went up on a mountain to pray**, and **He prayed to God** all night."*

Luke 6:12 (NLT)

*"And **I will pray the Father**, and **He shall give you** another Comforter, that He may abide with you for ever."*

John 14:16

ii. Jesus Prayed to the Heavenly Father in the Garden of Gethsemane

*"He went a little farther and fell on His face, and **prayed, saying, "O My Father**, if it is possible, let this cup pass from Me; nevertheless, not as I will, but as You will."*

Matthew 26:39 (NKJV)

*"Again, **a second time, He** went away and **prayed**, saying, "O **My Father**, if this cup cannot pass away from Me unless I drink it, Your will be done."*

Matthew 26:42 (NKJV)

*"But **Jesus said** to him…Or **do you think that I cannot now pray to My Father**, and He will provide Me with more than twelve legions of angels?*

Matthew 26:52-53 (NKJV)

*"**Jesus**…took the five loaves and two fish, **lifted His face to heaven in prayer**, blessed, broke, and gave the bread to the disciples."*

Matthew 14:18-21 (MSG)

iii. Jesus Prayed to the Heavenly Father Before the Miracle of Feeding the Five Thousand with 5 Loaves and 2 Fishes

*"**Then Jesus took the loaves, gave thanks to God**, and distributed them to the people. Afterward He did*

the same with the fish. And they all ate as much as they wanted."

John 6:11 (NLT)

iv. **In what is appropriately called the Lord's Prayer in John chapter 17, Jesus Prayed to the Heavenly Father for Himself, His Disciples and for All Believers**

*"**Jesus** spoke these words, **lifted up His eyes to heaven, and said:** "Father, the hour has come. Glorify Your Son, that Your Son also may glorify You."*

John 17:1 (NKJV)

*"And now, **O Father, glorify Me** together with Yourself, with the glory which I had with You before the world was."*

John 17:5 (NKJV)

v. **Jesus Prayed to the Heavenly Father for His Disciples**

*"…**Holy Father**, keep through Your name those whom You have given Me, that they may be one as We are."*

John 17:11 (NKJV)

vi. **Jesus Prayed to the Heavenly Father for All Believers**

*"I do not **pray for these alone, but also for those who will believe in Me through their word; that they all may be one**, as You, **Father**, are in Me, and I in You;*

that they also may be one in Us, that the world may believe that You sent Me."

John 11:41-42 (NKJV)

"**Father**, I desire that they also whom You gave Me may be with Me where I am, that they may behold My glory which You have given Me…"

John 17:24 (NKJV)

"O **righteous Father**! *The world has not known You, but I have known You; and these have known that You sent Me.*

John 17:25 (NKJV)

vii. Jesus Prayed to the Heavenly Father as He Raised Lazarus from the Dead

*"…And **Jesus lifted up His eyes and said, "Father, I thank You that You have heard Me**. And I know that **You always hear Me**, but because of the people who are standing by I said this, that they may believe that You sent Me."*

John 11:41-42 (NKJV)

viii. Jesus Prayed to the Heavenly Father while on the Cross

*"Then **Jesus** said, "**Father, forgive them**, for they do not know what they do…"*

Luke 23:34 (NKJV)

"...*Jesus*...cried out with a loud voice...*"Father*, 'into Your hands I commit My spirit..."

Luke 23:46 (NKJV)

ix. Jesus Christ is now at the Right Hand of God the Father, interceding for us.

"...*It is Christ who died, and furthermore is also risen, who is even at the right hand of God, Who also makes intercession for us*.

Romans 8:34 (NKJV)

"**Christ Jesus** is the One Who died [to pay our penalty], and more than that, Who was raised [from the dead], and Who **is at the right hand of God interceding [with the Father] for us**."

Romans 8:34 (AMP)

c. God the Father Sends Answers to Our Prayers

Jesus said,

"But **the Comforter**, which is **the Holy Ghost, whom the FATHER will SEND in My name**, He shall teach you all things, and bring all things to your remembrance, whatsoever I have said unto you."

John 14:26

*"And **I will ask the Father**, and **He will give you** another Helper (Comforter, Advocate, Intercessor - Counselor, Strengthener, Standby), to be with you forever."*

John 14:16 (AMP)

2. Pray in the Name of Jesus

The number one reason why you must pray in the name of Jesus is that, it is the approved name that God Almighty has ordained. It is the only name that God has Given. It is the only name that is Above every other name in heaven, on earth and under the earth.

*"Therefore **GOD** also **has HIGHLY EXALTED Him** and **GIVEN Him THE NAME** which is ABOVE EVERY NAME, that **at the name of Jesus every knee should bow**, of those in heaven, and of those on earth, and of those under the earth, and that **every tongue should confess that Jesus Christ is Lord**, to the glory of God the Father."*

Philippians 2:9-11 (NKJV)

*"For this reason also [because He obeyed and so completely humbled Himself], **God has highly exalted Him and bestowed on Him the Name which is above every name**, so that at the name of Jesus every knee shall bow [in submission], of those who are in heaven and on earth and under the

earth, and that every tongue will confess and openly acknowledge that Jesus Christ is Lord (sovereign God), to the glory of God the Father."

Philippians 2:9-11 (AMP)

"Therefore, **God elevated Him** to the **place of highest honour** and **gave Him the name above all other names**, that AT THE NAME OF JESUS every knee should bow, in heaven and on earth and under the earth, and every tongue declare that Jesus Christ is Lord, to the glory of God the Father."

Philippians 2:9-11 (NLT)

"…by **the name of Jesus Christ of Nazareth**…whom God raised from the dead…Neither is there salvation in any other: **for there is none other name under heaven given among men**, whereby we must be saved."

Acts 4:10-12

Jesus Christ Himself said,

"And **whatsoever ye shall ask in My Name**, that will I do, that the Father may be glorified in the Son."

John 14:13

"Until now **you have asked nothing in My name. Ask**, and you will receive, that your joy may be full"

John 16:24 (NKJV)

*"In that day you will **ask in My name**..."*
John 16:26 (NKJV)

CASE STUDY 7:
A Lame Man is Miraculously Healed 'in the Name of JESUS'

"Now **Peter** and **John** went up together to the temple at the hour of prayer, the ninth hour. And a certain man lame from his mother's womb was carried, whom they laid daily at the gate of the temple which is called Beautiful, to ask alms from those who entered the temple; who, seeing Peter and John about to go into the temple, asked for alms. And fixing his eyes on him, with John, Peter said, "Look at us." So he gave them his attention, expecting to receive something from them.

Then Peter said, "Silver and gold I do not have, but what I do have I give you: In the name of Jesus Christ of Nazareth, rise up and walk."And he took him by the right hand and lifted him up, and immediately his feet and ankle bones received strength.

So he, leaping up, stood and walked and entered the temple with them—walking, leaping, and praising God. And all the people saw him walking and praising God. Then they knew that it was he who sat begging alms at the Beautiful Gate of the temple; and they were filled with wonder and amazement at what had happened to him.

Acts 3:1-10 (NKJV)

3. Repent of your Sins and Confess them to God

Prayer can be rendered ineffective and may not be answered due to sin. Sin is a great hindrance to prayer. It is therefore important to remove every hindrance to your prayers by dealing with the barrier of sin appropriately. Let us consider what the Bible teaches:

a. Sin Hinders Prayer

The Bible says,

"...the Lord's hand is not shortened, that it cannot save; neither His ear heavy, that it cannot hear: But YOUR INIQUITIES have SEPARATED BETWEEN YOU AND YOUR GOD, and YOUR SINS have HID HIS FACE from you, THAT HE WILL NOT HEAR.

Isaiah 59:1-2

"...the Lord's hand is not so short That it cannot save, Nor His ear so impaired That it cannot hear. But your wickedness has separated you from your God, And your sins have hidden His face from you so that He does not hear."

Isaiah 59:1-2 (AMP)

*"Listen! The Lord's arm is not too weak to save you, nor is his ear too deaf to **hear you call**. It's your sins that have cut you off from God. Because of your sins, He has turned away and will not listen anymore."*

Isaiah 59:1-2 (NLT)

"Look! Listen! God's arm is not amputated—He can still save. God's ears are not stopped up—He can still hear. *There's nothing wrong with God; the wrong is in you. Your wrongheaded lives caused the split between you and God. Your sins got between you so that He doesn't hear.* Your hands are drenched in blood, your fingers dripping with guilt, Your lips smeared with lies, your tongue swollen from muttering obscenities. No one speaks up for the right, no one deals fairly. They trust in illusion, they tell lies, they get pregnant with mischief and have sin-babies. …They weave wickedness, they hatch violence. They compete in the race to do evil and run to be the first to murder. They plan and plot evil, think and breathe evil, and leave a trail of wrecked lives behind them…"

Isaiah 59:1-2 (MSG)

CASE STUDY 8: JESUS

JESUS bore the sins of the world as He dies on the Cross, at that point, *He felt forsaken by God the Father.* Jesus laid down His life and was crucified for our sins. He committed no sin. (John 3:16).

"And about the ninth hour **Jesus cried out** with a loud voice, saying, "Eli, Eli, lama sabachthani?" that is, "**My God, My God, why have You forsaken Me?**
Matthew 27:46 (NKJV)

WHY?
This is the Reason:

"…O Lord my God, my Holy One… **You** are of **purer eyes** than to **behold evil**, And **cannot look on** wickedness…"
Habakkuk 1:12-13 (NKJV)

The key point is that, sin (un-repented of, and not confessed to God for forgiveness) is a major hindrance to prayer and can make you feel forsaken by God as the Scriptures say in Isaiah chapter 59:

"Behold, the Lord's hand is not shortened, that it cannot save; neither His ear heavy, that it cannot hear: But your iniquities have separated between you and your God, and your sins have hid His face from you, that He will not hear."
Isaiah 59:1-2

b. If You Cover Your Sin, You Will Not Prosper

"He that **covereth his sins** shall **not prosper**: but whoso **confesseth** and **forsaketh** them **shall** have **mercy**."

Proverbs 28:13

"He who **conceals** his **transgressions** will **not prosper**, But whoever **confesses** and **turns away from his sins** will find compassion and **mercy**."

Proverbs 28:13 (AMP)

"People who **conceal** their **sins will not prosper**, but **if they confess** and **turn from them**, they will **receive mercy**."

Proverbs 28:13 (NLT)

"You can't whitewash your sins and get by with it; **you find mercy by admitting** and **leaving them**."

Proverbs 28:13 (MSG)

c. Sin Can Hinder Prayer, Divine Healing and Restoration

The Lord says,

"If My people, which are called by My name, shall humble themselves, and **pray**, and seek my face, and TURN from their wicked ways; then will I HEAR from heaven, and will FORGIVE their SIN, and will HEAL their land."

2 Chronicles 7:14

"Then if My people who are called by My name will humble themselves and **PRAY** and seek my face and TURN from their wicked ways, I will HEAR from heaven and will FORGIVE their SINS and RESTORE their land."

2 Chronicles 7:14 (NLT)

"...My people, who are called by My Name, humble themselves, and **PRAY** and seek (crave, require as a necessity) My face and **TURN from their wicked ways**, then **I will HEAR** [them] from heaven, and **FORGIVE their SIN** and **HEAL their land.**"

2 Chronicles 7:14 (AMP)

"If...My God-defined people, respond by humbling themselves, **praying**, seeking my presence, and **turning their backs on their wicked lives, I'll be there ready for you: I'll listen** from heaven, **forgive their sins**, and **restore** their land to health."

2 Chronicles 7:13-14 (MSG)

The Psalmist said,

"*If I regard* **INIQUITY *in my heart***, *the* **LORD WILL NOT HEAR** *me.*"

Psalm 66:18

"***If I regard* SIN** *and* **BASENESS** *in my* **HEART** *[that is, if I know it is there and do nothing about it]*, **The Lord** *will* **NOT HEAR** *[me]*"

Psalm 66:18 (AMP)

"*If I had not confessed the sin* *in my heart*, *the Lord would* NOT *have* **listened**."

Psalm 66:18 (NLT)

4. Pray with Humility of Heart

God says,

"…*if My people who are called by My name will* **HUMBLE THEMSELVES** *and* **PRAY** *and seek My face and turn from their wicked ways*, **I will HEAR** *from heaven and will forgive their sins and restore their land.*"

2 Chronicles 7:14 (NLT)

"If My people, which are called by My name, **shall HUMBLE THEMSELVES**, and **PRAY**, and seek My face, and turn from their wicked ways; **THEN** will **I HEAR from heaven**, and will **forgive their sin**, and will **heal their land**."

2 Chronicles 7:14

"If…my God-defined people, **respond by humbling themselves, praying**, seeking My presence, and turning their backs on their wicked lives, **I'll be there ready for you: I'll listen from heaven, forgive their sins, and restore their land to health.**"

2 Chronicles 7:14-18 (MSG)

"…God resisteth **the proud**, but **giveth grace** unto **the humble**."

James 4:6

"…God is opposed to **the proud** and haughty, but [continually] **gives [the gift of] grace to the humble** [who turn away from self-righteousness]."

James 4:6 (AMP)

"…As the Scriptures say, **God opposes the proud** but **gives grace to the humble**."

James 4:6 (NLT)

"**Submit** yourselves therefore **to God**. Resist the devil, and he will flee from you."

James 4:7

"So **humble yourselves before God**. Resist the devil, and he will flee from you."

James 4:7 (NLT)

"So **submit to [the authority of] God**. Resist the devil [stand firm against him] and he will flee from you."

James 4:7 (AMP)

"...be **clothed with humility**: for God resisteth the proud, and **giveth grace** to **the humble**.

1 Peter 5:5

"...for **God is opposed to the proud** [the disdainful, the presumptuous, and He defeats them], but **He gives grace to the humble**.

1 Peter 5:5 (AMP)

"...**God** opposes the proud but **gives grace to the humble**."

1 Peter 5:5 (NLT)

CASE STUDY 9:
Jesus Spoke about the Proud Pharisee and the Humble Tax Collector

"He also told this parable to some people who trusted in themselves and were confident that they were righteous [posing outwardly as upright and in right standing with God], and who viewed others with contempt:

"Two men went up into the temple [enclosure] to pray, one **a Pharisee** and the other a tax collector.

The Pharisee stood [ostentatiously] and began praying to himself [in a self-righteous way, saying]: 'God, I thank You that I am not like the rest of men—swindlers, unjust (dishonest), adulterers—or even like this tax collector. I fast twice a week; I pay tithes of all that I get.' But **the tax collector, standing at a distance, would not even raise his eyes toward heaven**, but was **striking his chest [in humility** and **repentance]**, saying, **'God, be merciful and gracious to me, the** [especially wicked] **sinner [that I am]**!' I tell you, this man went to his home justified [forgiven of the guilt of sin and placed in right standing with God] rather than the other man; for EVERYONE WHO EXALTS HIMSELF WILL BE HUMBLED, but HE WHO HUMBLES HIMSELF [forsaking SELF-RIGHTEOUS PRIDE] WILL be EXALTED."

Luke 18:9-14 (AMP)

5. Be Guided and Led by the Holy Spirit in Prayer.

The Bible says,

> "For all who are **led by the Spirit of God** are children of God."

Romans 8:14 (NLT)

"For as many as are **led by the Spirit of God**, they are the sons of God."

Romans 8:14

"For all who are **allowing themselves to be led by the Spirit of God** are sons of God."

Romans 8:14 (AMP)

6. Pray by the Power of the Holy Spirit and Pray in the Spirit

"...**the SPIRIT** also **helpeth** our infirmities: for **we know not what we should pray for as we ought:** but **the SPIRIT...maketh intercession for us** with groanings which cannot be uttered. And **He that searcheth the hearts knoweth what is the mind of the SPIRIT**, because **He maketh intercession** for the saints **according to the will of God.**"

Romans 8:26-27

"...**the SPIRIT** [comes to us and] **helps us** in our weakness. **We do not know what prayer to offer or how to offer it as we should, but the SPIRIT Himself** [knows our need and at the right time] **intercedes on our behalf** with sighs and groanings too deep for words. And He Who searches the hearts knows what the mind of the SPIRIT is, because **the**

SPIRIT intercedes [before God] **on behalf of God's people in accordance with God's will."**
        Romans 8:26-27 (AMP)

"…*the* **HOLY SPIRIT HELPS US** *in our weakness… we don't know what God wants us to pray for. But the* **HOLY SPIRIT PRAYS FOR US** *with groanings that cannot be expressed in words. And* **the Father Who knows all hearts knows what the SPIRIT is saying, for THE SPIRIT PLEADS FOR US believers in harmony with God's own will.**"
        Romans 8:26-27 (NLT)

"**With all prayer** *and petition* **PRAY** *[with specific requests] at all times [on every occasion and in every season]* **IN THE SPIRIT…**"
        Ephesians 6:18 (AMP)

"**PRAYING** *always with* **all prayer** *and supplication* **IN THE SPIRIT…**"
        Ephesians 6:18 (NLT)

"**PRAY IN THE SPIRIT at all times** *and on every occasion. Stay alert and be persistent in your prayers for all believers everywhere.*"
        Ephesians 6:18

7. Pray in Faith, by Faith, with Faith in God

The Scripture says,

*"...it is impossible to please God without **FAITH**. Anyone who wants to come to Him must **believe that God exists** and that **He rewards those who sincerely seek Him**."*

Hebrews 11:6 (NLT)

*"...**without FAITH it is impossible to please Him**: for he that cometh to God must **believe that He is**, and that **He is a rewarder** of them that diligently seek Him.*

Hebrews 11:6

*"...**without FAITH it is impossible to** [walk with God and] **please Him**, for whoever comes [near] to God must [necessarily] **believe that God exists** and that **He rewards those who** [earnestly and diligently] **seek Him**."*

Hebrews 11:6 (AMP)

"It's impossible to please God apart from FAITH. And why? Because anyone who wants to approach God must believe both that He exists and that He cares enough to respond to those who seek Him."

Hebrews 11:6 (MSG)

8. Pray Believing Prayers

Jesus said,

"*...**whosoever shall say** unto this mountain, Be thou removed, and be thou cast into the sea; **and SHALL NOT DOUBT in his heart,** but **shall BELIEVE** that those things which **he saith shall come to pass; he shall have whatsoever he saith.**"

Mark 11:23

"*...**you can say to this mountain,** 'May you be lifted up and thrown into the sea,' and it will happen. But **YOU MUST REALLY BELIEVE it will happen** and **HAVE NO DOUBT** in your heart.*"

Mark 11:23 (NLT)

"*...**whoever says** to this mountain, 'Be lifted up and thrown into the sea!' and **DOES NOT DOUBT** in his heart **[in God's unlimited power]**, but **BELIEVES** that what he says is going to take place, **it will be done for him** [in accordance with God's will].*"

Mark 11:23 (AMP)

"*...What things soever ye desire, when ye pray, **BELIEVE** that **ye receive them,** and **ye shall have them.**"

Mark 11:24

"*...**you can pray for anything**, and **if you BELIEVE** that you've received it, **it will be yours.**"

Mark 11: 24 (NLT)

"...whatever things you **ask for in prayer** *[in accordance with God's will]*, **BELIEVE** *[with confident trust]* that you have received them, and **they will be given to you**."

Mark 11: 24 (AMP)

9. Pray and Believe God's Rewards for Faithful Intercession

"...*GOD...is a REWARDER of them that* **diligently seek Him**."

Hebrews 11:6

"...***GOD...REWARDS*** those who *[**earnestly** and **diligently**] seek Him*."

Hebrews 11:6 (AMP)

"...***GOD...REWARDS*** those who **sincerely seek Him**."

Hebrews 11:6 (NLT)

"For God is not unrighteous to **forget your work** and **labour of love**, which ye have shewed toward His name, in that **ye have ministered to the saints, and do minister**."

Hebrews 6:10

"For **God is not unjust** so as **to forget your work** and the **love which you have shown for His name in ministering** to [**the needs of**] the saints (**God's people**), as you do."

Hebrews 6:10 (AMP)

"For **God** is not unjust. He **will not forget how hard you have worked for Him** and **how you have shown your love to Him by caring for other believers**, as you still do."

Hebrews 6:10 (NLT)

"God doesn't miss anything. **He knows perfectly well all the love you've shown Him by helping needy Christians**, and that you keep at it."

Hebrews 6:10-12 (MSG)

10. Pray Persistently. Don't Give Up.

- Never get tired of praying.
- Never give up prayer for anything.
- There is no substitute for prayer when it comes to asking and receiving things from God.
- There is no substitute for prayer when it comes to standing in the gap for God's people and God's Kingdom Business.

- Never stop trusting God with your prayers, no matter how small or great you may consider your prayers to be.
- Prayer works, so pray, and pray, and pray, until you have prayed and pray persistently.

a. The Persistent Widow's Request Was Granted

"One day **Jesus told His disciples a story** to show that they should **ALWAYS PRAY and NEVER GIVE UP.** "There was a judge in a certain city," He said, "who neither feared God nor cared about people. **A widow** of that city came to him **repeatedly**, saying, 'Give me justice in this dispute with my enemy.' **The judge ignored her for a while**, but finally he said to himself, 'I don't fear God or care about people, but this woman is driving me crazy. **I'm going to see that she gets justice, because she is wearing me out with her constant requests!'"**

Then the Lord said, **"Learn a lesson from this unjust judge.** Even he rendered a just decision in the end. **So don't you think God will surely give justice to His chosen people who cry out to him day and night?** Will He keep putting them off? I tell you, **He will grant justice to them quickly!** But when the Son of Man returns, how many will He find on the earth who have faith?"

Luke 18:1-8 (NLT)

b. The Persistent Knocker Received Bread

"It happened that while *Jesus was praying* in a certain place, after He finished, one of His disciples said to Him, "Lord, teach us to pray just as John also taught his disciples."...

Then He said to them, *"Suppose one of you has a friend, and goes to him at* **midnight** *and says, 'Friend, lend me* **three loaves [of bread]**; *for a friend of mine who is on a journey has just come to visit me, and I have nothing to serve him'; and from inside he answers, 'Do not bother me; the door has already been shut and my children and I are in bed; I cannot get up and give you anything.' I tell you, even though he will not get up and give him anything just because he is his friend, yet **BECAUSE OF HIS PERSISTENCE and boldness HE WILL GET up and give him WHATEVER HE NEEDS.***

"So I say to you, ask and keep on asking, and it will be given to you; seek and keep on seeking, and you will find; knock and keep on knocking, and the door will be opened to you. *For EVERYONE WHO KEEPS on ASKING [PERSISTENTLY], RECEIVES; and HE WHO KEEPS on SEEKING [PERSISTENTLY], FINDS; and to HIM WHO KEEPS on KNOCKING [PERSISTENTLY], the DOOR will be OPENED.*

What father among you, if his son asks for a fish, will give him a snake instead of a fish? Or if he asks for an egg, will give him a scorpion? If you, then, being evil [that is, sinful by nature], know how to give good gifts to your children, how much more will your heavenly Father give the Holy Spirit to those who ask and continue to ask Him!"

Luke 11:1-13 (AMP)

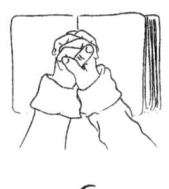

6

Things To Pray For

1. **Pray The Model Prayer**

   (**PRAY FOR**: the Kingdom of God, the Will of God, Daily bread, Forgiveness, Guidance, Victory over temptation and Deliverance from Evil).

   Jesus Christ taught us:

   *"After **this manner** therefore **PRAY ye**: Our Father which art in heaven, Hallowed be Thy name. THY KINGDOM Come, THY WILL BE Done in earth, as it is in heaven. GIVE US this day OUR DAILY BREAD. And FORGIVE US our debts, as we forgive our debtors. And LEAD US NOT INTO TEMPTATION, but DELIVER US FROM EVIL: For Thine is the kingdom, and the power, and the glory, for ever. Amen."*

   Matthew 6:9-13

2. **Pray for the Gifts of the Holy Spirit**

The Scriptures say,

"...***covet*** earnestly the **best** GIFTS..."

1 Corinthians 12:31

"...***earnestly desire*** the best GIFTS..."

1 Corinthians 12:31 (NKJV)

"...***earnestly desire*** and **strive for the greater** GIFTS [if acquiring them is going to be your goal]."

1 Corinthians 12:31 (AMP)

9 Gifts of the Holy Spirit You Could Pray for

"But the manifestation of the Spirit is given to each one for the profit of all: for to one is given **the word of wisdom** through the Spirit, to another **the word of knowledge** through the same Spirit, to another **faith** by the same Spirit, to another **gifts of healings** by the same Spirit, to another **the working of miracles**, to another **prophecy**, to another **discerning of spirits**, to another **different kinds of tongues**, to another **the interpretation of tongues**."

1 Corinthians 12:7-10 (NKJV)

You May Pray for these Other Gifts

"And God has appointed these in the church: first **apostles**, second **prophets**, third **teachers**, after that **miracles**, then **gifts of healings, helps, administrations, varieties of tongues**. Are all **apostles**? Are all **prophets**? Are all **teachers**? Are all **workers of miracles**? Do all have **gifts of healings**? Do all **speak with tongues**? Do all **interpret**?

1 Corinthians 12:28-30 (NKJV)

*"Pursue love, and **desire spiritual gifts**, but especially that you may prophesy.*

1 Corinthians 14:1 (NKJV)

You Could Pray for Other Ministry Gifts and Services

Since we have **gifts** that differ according to the **grace given to us**, each of us is to use them accordingly: if [someone has **the gift of] prophecy**, [let him speak a new message from God to His people] in proportion to the faith possessed; **if service, in the act of serving**; or **he who teaches, in the act of teaching**; or **he who encourages, in the act of encouragement; he who gives, with generosity**; he who **leads, with diligence; he who shows mercy [in caring for others]**, with cheerfulness.

Romans 12:6-8 (AMP)

*"Having then gifts differing according to the grace that is given to us, whether **prophecy**, let **us prophesy according to the proportion of faith**; Or ministry, let us wait on our ministering: or he that **teacheth, on teaching**; Or he that **exhorteth, on exhortation**: he that **giveth**, let him do it with simplicity; he that **ruleth, with diligence**; he that **sheweth mercy,** with cheerfulness.*

Romans 12:6-8 (KJV)

3. Pray for the Sick and the Afflicted

The Bible says,

*"Is any among you **afflicted? LET HIM PRAY**… Is any **sick** among you? **Let him call for the elders of the church; and LET THEM PRAY OVER HIM, anointing him with oil in the name of the Lord:***

*And **the PRAYER OF FAITH shall save the sick**, and **the Lord shall raise him up**; and if he have committed sins, they shall be forgiven him…and **PRAY ONE FOR ANOTHER**, that ye may be **healed**. The **EFFECTUAL FERVENT PRAYER** of a righteous man **availeth much**."*

James 5:13-16

"Is anyone among you **suffering**? He must **pray**…Is anyone among you sick? He must **call for the elders (spiritual leaders) of the church and** they are to **pray over him**, anointing him with oil in the name of the Lord; and the **prayer of faith** will **restore the one who is sick**, and the Lord will raise him up; and if he has committed sins, he will be forgiven. Therefore…**pray** for one another, that you may **be healed** and **restored**. The **heartfelt and persistent prayer** of a righteous man (believer) can accomplish much [when put into action and made effective by God—it is dynamic and can have **tremendous power**]."

James 5:13-16 (AMP)

4. PRAY FOR: all People, Kings, Leaders, all Those in Authority; your own Personal life, and the Salvation of Unsaved Loved Ones

*"I exhort therefore, that, first of all, **supplications, prayers, intercessions, and giving of thanks, be made for all men;** For **kings**, and **for all that are in authority**; that we may lead a quiet and peaceable life in all godliness and honesty. **For this is good and acceptable in the sight of God our Saviour;** Who will have **all men to be saved, and to come unto the knowledge of the truth**."*

1 Timothy 2:1-4

"…I urge that **petitions (specific requests), prayers, intercessions (prayers for others) and thanksgivings** be offered on **behalf of all people**, for **kings** and **all who are in [positions of] high authority**, so that we may live a peaceful and quiet life in all godliness and dignity. **This [kind** of praying] is good and acceptable and pleasing in the sight of God our Saviour**, who wishes **all people to be saved** and to come to the knowledge and recognition of the [divine] truth."

1 Timothy 2:1-4 (AMP)

5. Pray for Wisdom and Understanding

The Bible says,

*"**If any of you lacks WISDOM, let him ASK of God**, who gives to all liberally and without reproach, and **it will be given to him**."*

James 1:5 (NKJV)

King Solomon Prayed for Wisdom and Understanding. God Blessed Him with Wisdom, Understanding, Honour and Riches.

At Gibeon the Lord appeared to Solomon in a dream by night; and **God said, "Ask! What shall I give you?"**

And Solomon said: "You have shown great mercy to Your servant David my father, because he walked before You in truth, in righteousness, and in uprightness of heart with You; You have continued this great kindness for him, and You have given him a son to sit on his throne, as it is this day. Now, O Lord my God, You have made Your servant king instead of my father David, but I am a little child; I do not know how to go out or come in. And Your servant is in the midst of Your people whom You have chosen, a great people, too numerous to be numbered or counted. Therefore give to **Your servant an understanding heart** to judge Your people, **that I may discern between good and evil**. For who is able to judge this great people of Yours?"

The speech pleased the Lord, that Solomon had asked this thing. Then God said to him: **"Because you have asked this thing**, and have not asked long life for yourself, nor have asked riches for yourself, nor have asked the life of your enemies, but have asked for yourself understanding to discern justice, behold, **I have done according to your words; see, I HAVE GIVEN YOU a WISE and UNDERSTANDING HEART,** so that there has not been anyone like you before you, nor shall any like you arise after you. And **I have also given you what you have not asked: BOTH RICHES and HONOUR, so that there shall not be anyone like you among the kings all your days.** So if you walk in My ways, to keep My statutes and My commandments, as your father David walked, then I will lengthen your days."

1 Kings 3:5-14 (NKJV)

6. **Pray for Personal Safety**

a. **Ezra and the Jews Prayed for Personal Safety**

"Then ***I proclaimed a fast*** there at the river Ahava, so that we might **humble ourselves before our God to seek from Him a SAFE journey for us, our children, and all our possessions.** For I was ashamed **to request troops and horsemen from the king to PROTECT us from the ENEMY along the way...**"

Ezra 8:21-22 (AMP)

b. **Daniel Was a Man of Prayer Whose Safety in the Lion's Den Was Guaranteed by God's Angel**

"...***Daniel***...went home and **knelt down as usual** in his upstairs room, with its windows open toward Jerusalem. He *PRAYED THREE TIMES A DAY,* just **as he had always** done, giving thanks to his God. Then the officials went together to Daniel's house and found him *PRAYING AND ASKING FOR GOD'S HELP.* So they went straight to the king and reminded him about his law. "Did you not sign a law that for the next thirty days *ANY PERSON WHO PRAYS* to anyone, divine or human—except to you, Your Majesty—*WILL BE THROWN INTO THE DEN OF LIONS?*"

"Yes," the king replied, "that decision stands; it is an official law of the Medes and Persians that cannot be revoked."

Then they told the king, "That man *DANIEL*, one of the captives from Judah, is ignoring you and your law. He *STILL PRAYS TO HIS GOD THREE TIMES A DAY.*"

Hearing this, the king was deeply troubled, and he tried to think of a way to save Daniel. He spent the rest of the day looking for a way to get Daniel out of this predicament.

In the evening the men went together to the king and said, "Your Majesty, you know that according to the law of the Medes and the Persians, no law that the king signs can be changed."

So at last the king gave orders for *DANIEL* to be *ARRESTED AND THROWN INTO THE DEN OF LIONS*. The king said to him, "May your God, whom you serve so faithfully, rescue you."

Daniel 6:10-16 (NLT)

"Then the king returned to his palace and spent the night fasting. He refused his usual entertainment and couldn't sleep at all that night.

Very early the next morning, the king got up and hurried out to the lions' den. When he got there, he called out in anguish, **"Daniel, servant of the living God!** *Was your God, whom you serve so faithfully, able* **to rescue you from the lions?"**

Daniel answered, "Long live the king! **My God sent His angel to shut the lions' mouths so that they**

would not hurt me*, for I have been found innocent in his sight. And I have not wronged you, Your Majesty."*

The king *was overjoyed and **ordered** that **Daniel be lifted from the den**. **Not a scratch was found on him**, for he had trusted in his God."*

Daniel 6:10, 18-23 (NLT)

7. Pray that God Will Rescue and Deliver You from Evil and Wicked People

*"**Pray**, too, **that we will be rescued from wicked** and **evil people**, for not everyone is a believer. But the Lord is faithful; **He will strengthen you** and **guard you from the evil one**."*

2 Thessalonians 3:2-3 (NLT)

*"and [**pray**] that we will be **rescued from perverse and evil men**; for not everyone has the faith. But the Lord is faithful, and He will strengthen you [setting you on a firm foundation] and **will PROTECT and guard you from the evil one**."*

2 Thessalonians 3:2-3 (AMP)

*"...**Pray** that the Master's Word will simply take off and race through the country to a groundswell of response...And **PRAY that we'll be RESCUED from these scoundrels who are trying to do us in**. I'm finding that not all "believers" are believers. **But the Master***

never lets us down. He'll stick by you and PROTECT you from evil."

2 Thessalonians 3:2-3 (MSG)

"...**PRAY**...that **we may be delivered from unreasonable and wicked men**: for all men have not faith. But the Lord is faithful, who shall stablish you, and **keep you from evil.**"

2 Thessalonians 3:1-3

8. **Pray for those who despitefully use you and those who persecute you. Pray for your enemies**

Jesus said,

"But I say unto you, **Love your enemies, bless them that curse you, do good to them that hate you***, and* **PRAY** *for them which despitefully use you, and persecute you"*

Matthew 5:44

"You have heard the law that says the punishment must match the injury: 'An eye for an eye, and a tooth for a tooth.' But I say...**If someone slaps you on the right cheek, offer the other cheek also...** "You have heard the law that says, 'Love your neighbour' and hate your enemy. **But I say, love your enemies!**

PRAY for those who persecute you! In that way, you will be acting as true children of your Father in heaven. For He gives His sunlight to both the evil and the good, and He sends rain on the just and the unjust alike. If you love only those who love you, what reward is there for that?...If you are kind only to your friends, how are you different from anyone else? Even pagans do that. But you are to be perfect, even as your Father in heaven is perfect."

Matthew 5:38-48 (NLT)

9. Pray for Missionaries, Ministers of the Gospel and Church Leaders

"Let the **elders** that rule well be counted worthy of **double honour**, especially they who **labour in the word** and doctrine."

1 Timothy 5:17

"The elders who perform their **leadership duties** well are to be **considered worthy of double honour**... especially **those who work hard at preaching and teaching [the word of God** concerning eternal salvation through Christ]."

1 Timothy 5:17 (AMP)

10. Pray for Spiritual Blessings

Apostle Paul Prayed for these, saying:

"Therefore I also…do not cease to give thanks for you, making mention of you in **my PRAYERS**: that the God of our Lord Jesus Christ, the Father of glory, may give to you *the spirit of wisdom and revelation in the knowledge of Him, the eyes of your understanding being enlightened;* **that you may know what is the hope of His calling,** what are **the riches of the glory of His inheritance in the saints**, and what is **the exceeding greatness of His power** toward us who believe, according to **the working of His mighty power** which He worked in Christ when He raised Him from the dead and seated Him at His right hand in the heavenly places, far above all principality and power and might and dominion, and every name that is named, not only in this age but also in that which is to come…"

Ephesians 1:15-23 (NKJV)

11. Pray and Resist the devil

Jesus Christ clearly explains to us the agenda, purpose, vision, mission and plan of the devil, who is referred to here as 'the thief':

"The thief does not come except to steal, and to kill, and to destroy…"

John 10:10 (NKJV)

"The **thief's purpose** is **to steal** and **kill** and **destroy**…"

John 10:10 (NLT)

Satan is the believer's chief adversary who seeks to destroy you in every possible way:

"Be sober, be vigilant; because **your ADVERSARY the DEVIL, as a ROARING LION, walketh about, seeking whom he may devour: Whom RESIST stedfast** in the faith, knowing that the same afflictions are accomplished in your brethren that are in the world."

1 Peter 5:8-9 (KJV)

"Submit yourselves therefore to God. **Resist the devil**, and **he will flee from** you."

James 4:7

"So submit to [the authority of] God. **Resist the devil [stand firm against him]** and **he will flee** from you."

James 4:7 (AMP)

Jesus said,

"And I will give unto thee the KEYS of the KINGDOM OF HEAVEN: and **whatsoever** thou shalt BIND on EARTH shall be BOUND in HEAVEN: and **whatsoever** thou **SHALT** LOOSE on EARTH shall be LOOSED in HEAVEN."

Matthew 16:19

*"I will give you **the KEYS (authority) of the kingdom of heaven**; and whatever you **bind [forbid, declare to be improper** and **unlawful]** on earth will have [already] been bound in heaven, and whatever you **loose [permit, declare lawful]** on earth will have [already] been loosed in heaven."*

Matthew 16:19 (AMP)

Jesus emphasised,

*"Verily I say unto you, **Whatsoever ye** shall **bind** on **earth shall be bound in heaven**: and **whatsoever ye** shall **loose on earth** shall be **loosed in heaven**. Again I say unto you, That if two of you shall agree on earth as touching anything that they shall **ask, it shall be done for them of my Father** which is **in heaven**."*

Matthew 18:18-19

7

Biblical Conditions for Effective Fervent Prayer

1. Pray According to the Will of God

*"And He that searcheth the hearts knoweth what is the mind of the Spirit, because **He maketh intercession for the saints ACCORDING** to the **WILL OF GOD.**"*

Romans 8:27

"And He who searches the hearts knows what the mind of the Spirit is, because **the Spirit intercedes [before God]** on behalf of God's people IN ACCORDANCE WITH GOD'S WILL."

Romans 8:27 (AMP)

"And this is the confidence that we have in Him, that, **IF WE ASK ANY THING ACCORDING TO HIS WILL, HE HEARETH US:** And *if we know that **He hear us, whatsoever we ask,** we know that **we have the petitions that we desired of Him**.*"

1 John 5:14-15

Jesus Prayed According to the Will of God

Jesus prayed three times over in a very difficult situation, however, He was not seeking His own will, but the will of God the Father by saying: not my will, but Thine will be done.

"And He...fell on His face, and prayed, saying, O my Father, if it be possible, let this cup pass from me: nevertheless NOT AS I WILL, but as THOU WILT."

Matthew 26:39

When king Nebuchadnezzar became converted and caught a revelation of the greatness, power, might, majesty and supremacy of God Almighty, he decalared;

"And all the inhabitants of the earth are reputed as nothing: and **HE DOETH ACCORDING TO HIS WILL in the army of heaven**, and among the inhabitants of the *earth: and none can stay his hand, or say unto Him, What doest thou?*

Daniel 4:35

2. Pray from the Altar of Forgiveness

For our prayer to be heard and answered by the Lord, we need His mercies and forgiveness. Our lack of forgiveness, our unwillingness to forgive others, and our reluctance to forgive those who have trespassed against us is a major hindrance to effective prayers. We must always approach our holy, righteous, just, merciful and loving God from the Altar of forgiveness. We must first forgive other people who have offended us, hurt us, harmed us, sinned against us, as we also seek God's forgiveness for our sins, then God will hear and answer our prayers.

Why is Forgiveness Necessary?

"Now whom you forgive anything, I also forgive. For if indeed I have forgiven anything, I have forgiven that one for your sakes in the presence of Christ, *LEST SATAN SHOULD TAKE ADVANTAGE OF US; **for we are** NOT IGNORANT of HIS DEVICES.*"

2 Corinthians 2:10-11 (NKJV)

"And DO NOT GIVE THE DEVIL AN OPPORTUNITY [to lead you into sin by **holding a grudge**, or **nurturing anger**, or **harbouring resentment**, or **cultivating bitterness**]."

Ephesians 4:27 (AMP)

"NEITHER GIVE PLACE to the DEVIL."

Ephesians 4:27

"for anger gives A FOOTHOLD TO THE DEVIL."

Ephesians 4:27 (NLT)

"Go ahead and be angry. You do well to be angry—but don't use your anger as fuel for revenge. And don't stay angry. Don't go to bed angry. DON'T GIVE THE DEVIL THAT KIND OF FOOTHOLD IN YOUR LIFE."

Ephesians 4:26-27 (MSG)

Jesus said,

"And when ye stand **praying, FORGIVE, if ye have ought against any: that your Father also which is in heaven may forgive you your trespasses.** BUT IF YE DO NOT FORGIVE, NEITHER WILL YOUR FATHER WHICH IS IN HEAVEN FORGIVE YOUR TRESPASSES."

Mark 11:25-26

"Whenever you stand **praying, if you have anything against anyone**, FORGIVE him [drop

the issue, let it go], so that your Father Who is in heaven will also forgive you your transgressions and wrongdoings [against Him and others]. But if **you do not forgive, neither will your Father in heaven forgive your transgressions."]"**

Mark 11:25-26 (AMP)

How to Forgive

"Let all bitterness, and wrath, and anger, and clamour, and evil speaking, be put away from you, with all malice: And be ye kind one to another, tender-hearted, ***FORGIVING ONE ANOTHER, EVEN AS GOD FOR CHRIST'S SAKE HATH FORGIVEN YOU.***

Ephesians 4:31-32

"Get rid of all bitterness, rage, anger, harsh words, and slander, as well as all types of evil behaviour. Instead, be kind to each other, tender-hearted, *forgiving one another, just as God through Christ has forgiven you.*"

Ephesians 4:31-32 (NLT)

"Make a clean break with all cutting, backbiting, profane talk. Be gentle with one another, sensitive. *Forgive one another as quickly and thoroughly as God in Christ forgave you.*"

Ephesians 4:31-32 (MSG)

3. Pray in Faith

"But he MUST ASK…IN FAITH, **without doubting [God's willingness to help]**, *for the one who doubts is like a billowing surge of the sea that is blown about and tossed by the wind. FOR SUCH A PERSON OUGHT NOT TO THINK OR EXPECT THAT HE WILL RECEIVE ANYTHING [AT ALL] FROM THE LORD.*"

James 1:6-7 (AMP)

"But let him ASK IN FAITH, **nothing wavering**. For he that wavereth is like a wave of the sea driven with the wind and tossed. For l**et not that man think that he shall receive any thing of the Lord.**"

James 1:6-7

"…**pray to the Father**. He loves to help. You'll get His help, and won't be condescended to when you ask for it. **ASK boldly, BELIEVINGLY, without a second thought**. People who "worry their prayers" are like wind-whipped waves. **Don't think you're going to get anything from the Master that way**, adrift at sea, keeping all your options open."

James 1:5-8 (MSG)

"But when you **ASK** Him, **be sure that your FAITH is IN GOD ALONE.** Do not waver, for a person with divided loyalty is as unsettled as a wave of the sea that is blown and tossed by the wind. **Such people should not expect to receive anything from the Lord.**"

James 1:6-7 (NLT)

Jesus said,

"…whosoever shall say unto this mountain, Be thou removed, and be thou cast into the sea; and **shall NOT DOUBT in his heart, but shall BELIEVE that those things which he saith shall come to pass; he shall have whatsoever he saith**. Therefore I say unto you, What things soever ye desire, **WHEN YE PRAY, BELIEVE** that ye receive them, **and ye shall have them**.

Mark 11:23-24

The Prayer of Faith

"And **the PRAYER OF FAITH** shall save the sick, and the Lord shall raise him up; and if he have committed sins, they shall be forgiven him."

James 5:15

Elijah Engaged the Prayer of Faith and God did Miracles

"**Elijah...prayed earnestly** that it would not rain; and it did not rain on the land for three years and six months. And **he prayed again**, and the heaven gave rain, and the earth produced its fruit."

James 5:17-18

"**Elijah** was a man with a nature like ours [with the same physical, mental, and spiritual limitations and shortcomings], and **he prayed intensely** for it not to rain, and it did not rain on the earth for three years and six months. Then **he prayed again**, and the sky gave rain and the land produced its crops [as usual]."

James 5:17-18 (AMP)

"...The **prayer** of a person living right with God **is something powerful** to be reckoned with. *Elijah*, for instance, human just like us, **prayed hard that it wouldn't rain, and it didn't**—not a drop for three and a half years. Then he prayed that it would rain, and it did. The showers came and everything started growing again."

James 5:16-18 (MSG)

12. Live in Obedience to God. Obey God's Word & Answers are Guaranteed to Your Prayers

The Bible says,

"And WHATSOEVER we ASK, we RECEIVE of Him, <u>because</u> WE KEEP HIS COMMANDMENTS, and DO those THINGS THAT ARE PLEASING IN HIS SIGHT."

1 John 3:22

"and we **RECEIVE** from Him WHATEVER we ASK <u>because</u> WE [CAREFULLY AND CONSISTENTLY] KEEP HIS COMMANDMENTS and **do the things that are pleasing in His sight [habitually seeking to follow His plan for us].**

1 John 3:22 (AMP)

"And we will RECEIVE from Him WHATEVER WE ASK <u>because</u> WE OBEY HIM and DO THE THINGS THAT PLEASE HIM."

1 John 3:22 (NLT)

"We're able to stretch our hands out and **RECEIVE WHAT WE ASKED for** <u>because</u> **WE'RE DOING WHAT HE SAID, DOING WHAT PLEASES HIM."**

1 John 3:22 (MSG)

4. Abide in Christ and His Word

Jesus said,

"*If ye* **ABIDE** *in* **ME,** *and* **MY WORDS ABIDE** *in* **YOU, YE** *shall* **ASK WHAT YE WILL,** *and* **IT SHALL BE DONE** *unto you.*"

John 15:7

"**If you remain in Me and My words remain in you** [that is, if we are vitally united and My message lives in your heart], **ASK WHATEVER YOU WISH and IT WILL BE DONE** for you."

John 15:7 (AMP)

"*But* ***if you remain in Me*** *and* ***My words remain in you****, you may* **ASK FOR ANYTHING** *you want, and* **IT WILL BE GRANTED!**"

John 15:7 (NLT)

5. Pray in the Name of JESUS

Jesus said,

"*Hitherto have* **YE ASKED** *nothing* **IN MY NAME: ask,** *and* **ye shall receive**, *that your joy may be full.*"

John 16:24

"Until now you have NOT ASKED [the Father] for anything IN MY NAME; but now **ask** and keep on asking and **you will receive**, so that your joy may be full and complete."

John 16:24 (AMP)

*"**Ask, USING MY NAME**, and **you will receive**, and you will have abundant joy."*

John 16:24

*"...Ask the Father for whatever...**ASK IN MY NAME**, according to My will, and **HE'LL MOST CERTAINLY GIVE IT TO YOU**. Your joy will be a river overflowing its banks!"*

John 16:23-24 (MSG)

13. Pray in the Spirit

- Praying in the Spirit means praying in tongues or in unknown tongues.
- This is one of God's precious and amazing signs and spiritual GIFTS for all those who believe in Jesus Christ as their personal Lord and Saviour.
- The gift of speaking in tongues is a prayer-language which God gives to all His children to communicate with Him in prayer.

After His resurrection, Our Lord Jesus Christ made this powerful declaration and promise:

"*...these SIGNS will follow* **those who believe: In My name** they will cast out demons; **THEY WILL SPEAK with NEW TONGUES**"

Mark 16:17

"**These signs** will accompany **those who have believed: in My name** they will cast out demons, **THEY WILL SPEAK in NEW TONGUES.**"

Mark 16:17 (AMP)

"*These are some of the* **signs that will accompany believers...in My name, THEY WILL SPEAK in NEW TONGUES**"

Mark 16:17 (MSG)

"*These* **miraculous signs** *will accompany those who* **believe**: *They will cast out demons* **in my name**, *and* **THEY WILL SPEAK in NEW LANGUAGES.**"

Mark 16:17 (NLT)

The Apostles and Disciples of Jesus Experienced this on the Day of Pentecost

"When the **Day of Pentecost** had fully come, they were all with one accord in one place. ...*And they were all filled* with *the Holy Spirit and began to* *speak with OTHER TONGUES, as the Spirit gave them utterance."*

Acts 2:1-4 (NKJV)

"And **they were all filled** [that is, diffused throughout their being] with **the Holy Spirit** and **began** to SPEAK in OTHER TONGUES (DIFFERENT LANGUAGES), as **the Spirit was giving them the ability to speak out [clearly and appropriately]**."

Acts 2:1-4 (AMP)

"…the **Holy Spirit** spread through their ranks, and *they started SPEAKING IN A NUMBER OF DIFFERENT LANGUAGES as the Spirit prompted them."*

Acts 2:1-4 (MSG)

"And everyone present was **filled with the Holy Spirit** and began *SPEAKING IN OTHER LANGUAGES, as the Holy Spirit gave them this ability."*

Acts 2:1-4 (NLT)

When the Apostles and Disciples of Jesus experienced the baptism of the Holy Spirit on the Day of Pentecost, they received supernatural ability to Pray in Tongues. Study the entire book of Acts 2:1-47 to have a clearer understanding of what happened on the Day of Pentecost with the outpouring of the Holy Spirit.

The Bible says,

"*But ye, beloved, building up yourselves…**praying in the Holy Ghost***"

Jude 1:20

"*But you, beloved, build yourselves up…**pray in the Holy Spirit***"

Jude 1:20 (AMP)

"*But you, dear friends…**pray in the power of the Holy Spirit***"

Jude 1:20 (NLT)

"*But you…build yourselves up…**by praying in the Holy Spirit***"

Jude 1:20 (MSG)

Apostle Paul said,

"*I thank my God, **I speak with tongues more than ye all***"

1 Corinthians 14:18

"*I thank God that **I speak in [unknown] tongues more than all of you***"

1 Corinthians 14:18 (AMP)

*"I'm grateful to God for **the gift of praying in tongues** that He gives us for praising Him, which leads to wonderful intimacies we enjoy with Him. **I enter into this as much or more than any of you.**"*

1 Corinthians 14:18 (MSG)

8

What is Fasting?

Fasting is a way of separating oneself from other things, in order to be before God's presence.

The Greek-root words from which fasting is derived include:

a. ńesteia (Vηστεια)

(nace –ti-ah) - Abstinence from food for religious purposes or spiritual reasons.

b. NESTEVO

Translated "Fast" is derived from 'NE' a negative prefix, and 'esthio', to eat.

Therefore, to *fast* basically means *not to eat*, (Abstaining from all food) solid or liquid.

- Take note, Satanists also fast (The Church of Satan).
- Occultists fast.
- Moslems fast for various reasons, during Ramadan, (the 9th month of the Moslem year).
- Human agents of the Devil also fast (Acts 23:12-22).

More Than 40 Men Bound Themselves Under a Curse to neither Eat nor Drink [to FAST] Till They Have Killed Paul

"And when it was day, **certain** of the **Jews banded together,** and **bound themselves under a curse, saying that** THEY WOULD NEITHER EAT NOR DRINK TILL THEY HAD KILLED PAUL.

"And **they were more than forty** which had made **this conspiracy**.

And they came to the chief priests and elders, and said, WE HAVE BOUND OURSELVES UNDER A GREAT CURSE, THAT WE WILL EAT NOTHING UNTIL WE HAVE SLAIN PAUL.

Now therefore ye with the council signify to the chief captain that he bring him down unto you to morrow, as though ye would enquire something more perfectly concerning him: **and we, or ever he come near, are READY TO KILL HIM.**

And when Paul's sister's son heard of their lying in wait, he went and entered into the castle, and told Paul.

Then Paul called one of the centurions unto him, and said, Bring this young man unto the chief captain: for he hath a certain thing to tell him.

So he took him, and brought him to the chief captain, and said, **Paul** the prisoner called me unto him, and **prayed** me to bring this young man unto thee, who hath something to say unto thee.

Then the chief captain took him by the hand, and went with him aside privately, and asked him, What is that thou hast to tell me?

And he said, The Jews have agreed to desire thee that thou wouldest bring down Paul to morrow into the council, as though they would enquire somewhat of him more perfectly.

But do not thou yield unto them: **for there lie in wait for him of them more than forty men, which have bound themselves with an oath,** that THEY WILL NEITHER EAT NOR DRINK TILL THEY HAVE KILLED HIM: and now are they ready, looking for a promise from thee.

So the chief captain then let the young man depart, and charged him, See thou tell no man that thou hast shewed these things to me."

Acts 23:12-22

9

What is Biblical Fasting?

Many people don't really know what it means to fast and pray biblically. It is not every fast that is biblical. Biblical fasting is entirely Scriptural or Bible-based fasting. Any fast which does not follow the principles of the Word of God is unacceptable to the Lord of the fast.

The Lord says in the book of Isaiah,

"Is this not the fast that I have chosen: To loose the bonds of wickedness, To undo the heavy burdens, To let the oppressed go free, And that you break every yoke?

Is it not to share your bread with the hungry, And that you bring to your house the poor who are cast out; When you see the naked, that you cover him, And not hide yourself from your own flesh?

Then your light shall break forth like the morning, Your healing shall spring forth speedily, And your righteousness shall go before you; The glory of the Lord shall be your rear guard.

Isaiah 58:6-8 (NKJV)

"Is not this the fast that I have chosen?

1. To loosen the bonds of wickedness, - v.6
2. To undo the bands of the yoke, and - v.6
3. To let the oppressed go free and - v.6
4. To break every yoke? - v.6
5. Is it not to divide your bread with the hungry, and bring the homeless poor into the house; When you see the naked, to cover him; and not to hide yourself from your own flesh?   - v.7
6. Then your light break out like the dawn - v.8
7. And your recovery will spring forth speedily; - v.8
8. And your righteousness will go before you;- v.8
9. The glory of the LORD will be your reward." - v.8

(Isaiah 58: 6-8)

A biblical definition of fasting is:

A Christian's voluntary and total abstinence from the natural carnal desires for godly and spiritual purposes of dedicating your time and your life to God, for:

1. Spiritual growth and development of your "inner man" (your spirit part).
2. The sharpening of your spiritual senses for exploits and spiritual warfare.
3. Fellowship with the Lord.
   - Biblical fasting sharpens prayer.
   - Biblical fasting moves the good hand of God on your behalf for the purpose of His Kingdom expansion.

In other words, it is:

Withdrawal from other things to spend quality time with the Lord.

In *biblical fasting*, a person may abstain from:

1. Food and Water (Luke 4:2 — Jesus, Esther 4:16- Esther, Mordecai and the Jews)
2. Food (solid or liquid)
3. Food and Sex (1 Corinthians 7:5) — In the case of married couples, just for the period of fasting.

During this period of prayer and fasting, by mutual consent, a husband or wife may abstain from his or her rights to *Legitimate Natural Enjoyment* in marriage, for the greater purpose of enjoying the presence of the Lord.

Biblical Fasting

By my count, there are 77 biblical references to fasting in the Scriptures.

Fasting is denial of self for a period of time in order to devote oneself to prayer.

- Normally, it is a denial of food.
- It could be a denial of other things which affect the body, such as sex in marriage, or the mind, such as non-Christian television programmes; or anything that keeps a person from placing concentrated attention on God.
- It is one's willingness to set aside legitimate appetites of the body and mind to concentrate on the work of scriptural praying, meditation, worship, and willingness to demonstrate that we are intensely seeking the Lord with all our heart and will not let God go, unless God answers us.

Biblical fasting is a discipline. By the act of fasting, you are voluntarily denying yourself for spiritual reasons.

- It must be God-centered.
- It is voluntary - fasting is not to be coerced.

- A broader view of fasting does not only always deal with abstinence from food.

Sometimes we may need to fast from:
- Involvement with other people, especially those who do not contribute to your spiritual upliftment.
- The mass media, i.e. – ungodly T.V. programmes, DVDs, Movies, Printed magazines, books and journals.
- Unnecessary telephone calls/ messaging/ internet/ social media activities.
- Unnecessary talking and conversations with people.

The above may be helpfully observed in order to become more absorbed in a time of spiritual activity and fellowship with the Lord.

- The Bible refers to fasting primarily in terms of abstinence from food, water and in some cases sex in marriage.
- Even though some people, for medical reasons, cannot fast, most of us should not overlook fasting's benefits in the disciplined pursuit of a Christ-like life.

Biblical fasting is a way of moving into a spiritual realm of faith and power by putting down (denying) our fleshly desires. The Holy Spirit and the spirit part of us takes dominance in moving in an area of scriptural prayer, (communion with God) that we cannot get into through any other way. Biblical fasting requires moving into the spirit, praying in the spirit and being in the spirit.

Fasting Without Food or/and Water

i. Jesus fasted without Food.

*"And **Jesus**…was led by the Spirit into the wilderness… **forty days**…And in those days **He did eat nothing:** and when they were ended, He afterward hungered."*

Luke 4:1-2

ii. Esther, Mordecai and the Jews Fasted without Food and water

Esther said to Mordecai,

*"Go, gather together **all the Jews**…and **fast** ye for me, and **neither eat nor drink three days, night or day: I also and my maidens will fast** likewise…"*

Esther 4:16

Withholding Sexual Relations in Marriage for Fasting & Prayer

The Bible says,

*"**DEFRAUD YE NOT one the other, EXCEPT** it be with consent for a time, **THAT YE may GIVE YOURSELVES** to **FASTING** and **PRAYER;** and **come together again, that Satan tempt you not** for your incontinency."*

1 Corinthians 7:5

"DO NOT DEPRIVE **each other [of marital rights]**, EXCEPT...by MUTUAL **CONSENT** for a time, so THAT YOU may DEVOTE YOURSELVES [UNHINDERED] to PRAYER, but **come together again so that Satan will not tempt you [to sin]** because of your lack of self-control."

1 Corinthians 7:5 (AMP)

*"**Do not deprive each other** OF SEXUAL relations, UNLESS you both agree to refrain from sexual intimacy for a limited time so you can GIVE YOURSELVES MORE COMPLETELY TO PRAYER. Afterward, you should **come together again so that Satan won't be able to tempt you** because of your lack of self-control."*

1 Corinthians 7:5 (NLT)

"...The marriage bed must be a place of mutuality—the husband seeking to satisfy his wife, the wife seeking to satisfy her husband. Marriage is not a place to "stand up for your rights." *Marriage is a decision to serve the other, whether in bed or out.* ABSTAINING FROM SEX IS PERMISSIBLE FOR A PERIOD OF TIME IF YOU BOTH AGREE TO IT, and IF IT'S FOR THE PURPOSES OF PRAYER AND FASTING—but only for such times. Then come back together again. Satan has an ingenious way of tempting us when we least expect it…"

1 Corinthians 7:5-6 (MSG)

BIBLICAL FASTING

F - **F**orsake our
A - **A**ppetite for a
S - **S**pecific
T - **T**ime frame for
I - *Intimacy with Spiritual*
N - *Nourishment from*
G - **God**

10

Types of Fasts

1. **Normal Fast** – *Abstaining from all Food, liquid or solid, but not from water, for any period of time. This can be undertaken as long as one disciplines him or herself before the Lord* (**Matthew 4:2; Luke 4:2**).

2. **Partial Fast** – *A limitation of the diet, but not abstention from all food* (**Daniel 1:12; Matthew 3:4**).

3. **Absolute or Complete Fast** – *Avoidance of all food and liquid, even water, for a period of time, for instance, a day, three days or one week* (**Ezra 10:6; Esther 4:16; Acts 9:9**).

4. **Supernatural Fast** – *This fast should only be undertaken by the Lord's specific calling, leading, direction, guidance and Miraculous Provision* (**Deuteronomy 9:9; 1 Kings 19:8**).

5. **Congregational Fast** – *A call for a sacred assembly, to gather the people and consecrate the assembly in worshipping God* (**Joel 2:15-16; Nehemiah 9:1; Esther 4:16; Acts 13:2**).

6. **National Fast** – *Calls for the entire nation or country to fast. During the early days of the United States of America, Congress proclaimed 3 national fasts* (**2 Chronicles 20:3; Acts 13:2**).

7. **Regular Fast** – *Every Jew was to fast on the Day of Atonement, an annual fast* (**Leviticus 16:29-31; Zechariah 8:19**).

8. **Occasional Fast** – *Occurs on special occasions on an 'as needed basis'* (**Matthew 9:15**)

Kinds of Fasts

1. The APOSTLE'S Fast

Purpose: For freedom from addiction to sin and from demonic oppression, sickness and disease (Matthew 17:14-21).

Jesus said to the 12 Apostles and Disciples,

*"However, **this kind does not go out EXCEPT by PRAYER and FASTING."***

Matthew 17:21 (NKJV)

2. The EZRA Fast – (A Fast for the Journey)

Purpose: For Solution to Complex and Difficult Problems (Ezra 8:21-23).

*"So we fasted and **entreated** our **God** for this, and He **answered** our prayer."*

Ezra 8:23 (NKJV)

To seek direction from the Lord for our lives, God's blessings upon our family and children; as well as God's provision for life.

6. The SAMUEL Fast

Purpose: For Evangelism

"So they gathered together at Mizpah, drew water, and poured it out before the Lord. And they fasted that day, and said there, "We have sinned against the Lord…"

1 Samuel 7:6 (NKJV)

7. The ELIJAH Fast

Purpose: For Solution to Emotional and Mental burn-out

*"So he [Elijah]…went in the strength of that food **forty days** and **forty nights**…"*

1 Kings 19:8 (NKJV)

8. The WIDOW'S Fast

Purpose: For the Provision of Physical Needs of others

"Is it not [the fast] to **share** *your* **bread** *with the* **hungry**...?"

Isaiah 58:7 (NKJV)

9. The APOSTLE PAUL'S Fast - (A 3 Day Fast)

Purpose: For Making Decisions with Insight and Wisdom

"And he was **three days** *without sight, and* **neither ate nor drank.**"

Acts 9:9 (NKJV)

10. The DANIEL Fast I – (A 10 Day Fast)

Purpose: For Physical Health or Healing

"Please test your servants for **ten days**, *and let them give us* **vegetables** *to eat and* **water** *to drink."*

Daniel 1:12 NKJV

11. The DANIEL Fast II – (21 Days Fast)

Purpose: To seek and understand God's vision, and to receive divine clarity and heavenly strategy for the fulfilment of God's purpose on earth.

"In those days I, Daniel, was mourning three full weeks. I ate no pleasant food, no meat or wine came into my mouth, nor did I anoint myself at all, till three whole weeks were fulfilled."

Daniel 10:2-3 (NKJV)

Eat no "pleasant food" (just vegetables, fruit and water).

3. The JOHN THE BAPTIST Fast

Purpose: For the Manifestation of your Testimony and Influence

*"...He will be great in the sight of the Lord, and shall drink neither wine nor strong drink. He will also be **filled** with the **Holy Spirit**, even from his mother's womb."*

Luke 1:15 (NKJV)

*"...his food was **locusts** and wild **honey**."*

Matthew 3:4 (NKJV)

4. The ESTHER Fast – (A 3 Day Fast)

Purpose: To Seek God in a time of Crisis or Trouble and for Spiritual Protection from the evil one.

*"...Gather all the Jews...fast for me; neither eat nor drink **for three days, night** or **day**. My maids and I will fast likewise..."*

Esther 4:16 (NKJV)

12. "The HUMBLING Fast"

Purpose: To withhold God's judgment on oneself or a loved one, and seeking God's mercy.

*"So it was, when Ahab heard those words, that he tore his clothes and put **sackcloth on his body**, and **fasted** and **lay in sackcloth**, and **went about mourning**.*

And the word of the Lord came to Elijah the Tishbite, saying, **"See how Ahab has humbled himself before Me? Because he has humbled himself before Me, I will not bring the calamity in his days.** *In the days of his son I will bring the calamity on his house."*

1 Kings 21:27-29 (NKJV)

Let us humble ourselves and intercede for someone in our families, workplace, community, church, village, town, city or country *"who knows better"* but isn't living it. The length and scope of this fast is determined by the Lord's leading.

13. The SINGLE PERSON'S Fast for Marriage

Purpose: To surrender to God, and seek God's will concerning marriage and the right person to marry (Genesis 24).

"Then the servant…departed…and went to Mesopotamia, to the city of Nahor. Then he said, O Lord God of my master Abraham, please give me success this day, and show kindness to my master Abraham.

And the man, wondering at her, remained silent so as to know whether the Lord had made his journey prosperous or not.

Then the man bowed down his head and worshiped the Lord. And he said, "Blessed be the Lord God of my master Abraham, who has not forsaken His mercy and His truth toward my master. As for me, being on the way, the Lord led me to the house of my master's brethren."

Food was set before him to eat, but he said, "I will not eat until I have told about my errand."

And he said, "Speak on."

Genesis 24:10, 12, 21, 26, 27, 33 (NKJV)

This is the first time *abstaining from food* is mentioned in the Bible.

14. The NATIONAL REVIVAL Fast

Purpose: To intercede for our nation and the nations of the world (Jonah 3:4-10; Nehemiah 1; Psalm 2:8)

The Lord says,

"Ask of Me, and I will give You The nations *for* Your inheritance, And the ends of the earth *for* Your possession."

Psalm 2:8 (NKJV)

The People of Nineveh Believed God and Proclaimed a National Fast

"And Jonah began to enter the city on the first day's walk. Then he cried out and said, "Yet forty days, and Nineveh shall be overthrown!"

So the people of Nineveh believed God, proclaimed a fast, *and put on sackcloth, from the greatest to the least of them.* Then word came to the king of Nineveh; and he arose from his throne and laid aside his robe, covered *himself* with sackcloth and sat in ashes. And he caused *it* to be proclaimed and published throughout Nineveh by the decree of the king and his nobles, saying,

Let neither man nor beast, herd nor flock, taste anything; do not let them eat, or drink water. *But let man and beast be covered with sackcloth, and cry mightily to God; yes,* **let everyone turn from his evil way** *and from the violence that is in his hands. Who can tell if God will turn and relent, and turn away from His fierce anger, so that we may not perish?*

Then God saw their works, that they turned from their evil way; and God relented from the disaster that He had said He would bring upon them, and He did not do it."

Jonah 3:4-10 (NKJV)

15. ONE DAY Fast

Purpose: One day set aside each year for self-examination and consecration (Leviticus 23:27 & Jeremiah 36:6)

"Also the tenth *day* of this seventh month *shall be* **the Day of Atonement**. It shall be **a holy convocation** for you…to the Lord."

Leviticus 23:27 (NKJV)

"You go, therefore, and **read from the scroll** which you have written at my instruction, **the words of the Lord**, in the hearing of the people in the Lord's house **on the day of fasting**. And you shall also read them in the hearing of all Judah who come from their cities."

Jeremiah 36:6 (NKJV)

16. The HEALING Fast

Purpose: For Healing miracles from God (Isaiah 58:1-9).

"Then your light shall break forth like the morning, ***Your healing shall spring forth speedily****, And your righteousness shall go before you; The glory of the Lord shall be your rear guard. Then you shall call, and the Lord will answer; You shall cry, and He will say, 'Here I am.'"*

Isaiah 58:8-9 (NKJV)

17. The 40 DAY Fast

Purpose: To seek God for greater sense of authority, as in Jesus' fast (Matthew 4:1-11; Luke 4:1, 2, 14-15, 22, 31-32).

1. **MOSES fasted 40 days and 40 nights when he went up to Mount Sinai for the first set of tablets from the LORD (Deuteronomy 9:9)**

    "When I was gone up into the mount to receive the tables of stone, even the tables of the covenant which the LORD made with you, then I abode in the mount ***forty days*** *and* ***forty nights, I neither did eat bread*** *nor* ***drink water:****"*

    Deuteronomy 9:9

2. MOSES fasted 40 days and 40 nights when he went up to Mount Sinai for the second set of the Ten Commandments from the LORD (Exodus 34:28)

"And he was there with the LORD **forty days** and **forty nights**; he did **neither eat bread, nor drink water**. And he wrote upon the tables the words of the covenant, the Ten Commandments."

Exodus 34:28

"And I fell down before the LORD, as at the first, **forty days** and **forty nights: I did neither eat bread**, nor **drink water**, because of all your sins which ye sinned, in doing wickedly in the sight of the LORD, to provoke Him to anger."

Deuteronomy 9:18

3. After ELIJAH had slain the prophets of Jezebel, he fled for his life to Mount Horeb, where he fasted 40 days and 40 nights (I Kings 19:8)

"And he arose, and did eat and drink, and went in the strength of that meat **forty days** and **forty nights** unto Horeb the mount of God."

I Kings 19:8

4. **JESUS fasted 40 days and 40 nights (Matthew 4:1-2)**

   *"Then was **Jesus** led up of the Spirit into the wilderness to be tempted of the devil. And when **He had fasted forty days** and **forty nights**, He was afterward an hungred."*

   Matthew 4:1-2

PowerPoint:

Try NOT to take on a major battle without fasting. For any new initiative, business, plan, or undertaking, it is very helpful to be clearly led by God.

At least, Fast until Evening, Seek God's Guidance in Taking Major Destiny Decisions (Judges 20:25-28)

"Then the children of Israel went up and **wept before the Lord until evening**, and *asked counsel of the Lord, saying, "Shall I again draw near for battle against the children of my brother Benjamin?"*

And the Lord said, "Go up against him."

Then all the children of Israel, that is, all the people, went up and came to the house of God and wept. **They sat there before the Lord and fasted**

that day until evening; and they offered burnt offerings and peace offerings before the Lord. So the children of Israel inquired of the Lord...saying, "Shall I yet again go out to battle against the children of my brother Benjamin, or shall I cease?"

And the Lord said, "Go up, for tomorrow I will deliver them into your hand."

Judges 20:25-28 (NKJV)

12

The Purpose of Fasting

Biblical Fasting is to be proclaimed for a purpose (Ephesians 2:1-10 & Titus 3:5-7)

- Fasting without a purpose renders it a miserable self-centered experience.
- There are many purposes for fasting given in the Bible.
- Whenever you fast, you should do so for at least one of these Biblical purposes.
- Fasting should *not* be used as a way to impress God in order to earn His acceptance.
- We are made acceptable to God through the work of Christ Jesus, *not* any of our works.

- Fasting has no eternal benefit for us until we come to God through repentance and faith.

18 Reasons For Biblical Fasting

Biblical Fasting is relevant today as it was in Old Testament times, as well as New Testament Apostolic times. However, fasting should be undertaken for the following purposes as guided by the Holy Scriptures and the Holy Spirit who authored them:

1. **To Strengthen Prayer** *(Ezra 8:23)*.
2. **To Seek God's Guidance** *(Judges 20; Acts 14:23)*.
3. **To Express Grief.** When *mourning and grieving* *(Judges 20:26; 1 Samuel 31:13; 2 Samuel 1:11-12; 1 Peter 3:18; 1 John 1:9)*.
4. **To Seek Deliverance and Protection** *(2 Chronicles 20:3-4; Ezra 8:21-23; Esther 4:16; Psalm 109)*.
5. **To Express Repentance and Return to God.** When *mourning and grieving* over sin; and there is need for *repentance* [Godly sorrowful for sin/ Deep Contrition] *(1 Samuel 7:6; Joel 2:12-15; Jonah 3:5-6; Nehemiah 9:1-3; Jeremiah 36:6-9)*
6. **To Humble Oneself Before God** for divine *intervention* in the circumstances of life *(1 Kings 21:27-20; Psalm 35:13; Luke 18:12)*.

7. **To Express Concern and Burden for the Work of God** *(Nehemiah 1:3-4; Daniel 9:3)*.
8. **To Minister to the Needs of Others** *(Isaiah 58: 6-7)*.
9. **To Overcome Temptation and Dedicate Yourself to God** *(Matthew 4:1-11)*.
10. **To Express Love and Worship to God** *(Luke 2:37; Zechariah 7:5)*.
11. **To *Hear* from God and Receive *direction* from Him** *(Exodus 34:27-28; 1 Kings 19:8; Acts 13:2-3; 14:23)*.
12. **When *mourning* for the Death of Loved Ones** *(1 Samuel 31:11-13)*.
13. **When *seeking* God's Protection, Favour and Blessing** on our lives, members of the church, families, community, village, town, city or nation *(Ezra 8:21-23)*.
14. **For God's *Deliverance* from Our Enemies** *(Psalm 35:13; Psalm 69:10; Psalm 109:24; 2 Chronicles 20:3)*.
15. **When God Stirs Our *Heart* to Fast in fulfilling His will** *(Isaiah 58; Matthew 17:21)*.
16. **To allow the Holy Spirit's *Full Control*** in our lives, education/career, marriage relationship, family, ministry, work, business, nations *(Acts 13:1-4)*.
17. **For the Holy Spirit to Give us *Revelation of our true Spiritual* Condition**, which results in our

brokenness, repentance, change of heart, mind and character.

18. **Biblical Fasting enables us to give Absolute Control** of our ***spirit, soul*** and ***body*** to the ***Holy Spirit***.

13

Things to Expect During Fasting

Through my little personal experience in fasting, as confirmed by scripture, there are some undesirable things one experiences during fasting. We should not be ignorant of them. Be informed, be mindful and be watchful. These things should not put you off. Expect them, so as to prepare adequately to cope with them/overcome them.

1. Hunger

- When fasting, expect the unpleasant and the unwelcome experience of hunger.
- This may be experienced at the initial stages of your fasting.
- Its aim is to defeat the goal of your fasting, to give you several reasons to stop or

discontinue your fast, and to break your fast earlier than scheduled or planned.
- Do not listen to the discouraging voice of the devil through the hunger.
- Do not give up, be not discouraged, press on fervently.
- The more you feel hungry, the more you need to pray, because that's when you are nearer to your answers, victory and breakthroughs.
- Discipline your eyes, your hands, your mouth, and your stomach.
- Do not yield to hunger. Stand strong and firm on your resolve to fast.
- Depend on the strength of the Holy Spirit (Zechariah 4:6).
- You can do all things through Christ who strengthens you (Philippians 4:13).
- Be an Overcomer. Do not live by bread (food) alone. (Matthew 4:2; Luke 4:2).

2. Temptation

During fasting, the devil, Satan, will try you and tempt you to sin (to do wrong, to go astray, to misbehave, to displease God, to indulge yourself) and by so doing losing the power, blessings and positive results and reward of your prayer and fasting.

- Jesus Himself was tempted during His fasting period, but, He overcame by quoting the scriptures related to the respective situations.
- This is because the devil knows that through fasting, you will be empowered, blessed and rewarded.
- Spend quality time Reading/Studying your Bible, memorize scriptures and quote them circumstantially when faced with temptations.
- Do not be unaware of temptations. Temptation is not sin. It becomes sin when we welcome it, yield to it, dwell on it, and enjoy its pleasure.
- If you yield to temptation by committing and practicing sin, you lose the glory of God which has been ordained for that period of waiting upon the Lord; as a result, your goal, objective and purpose will be defeated (Matthew 4:1-11; Luke 4:1-13).

> *"Yield not to temptation, for yielding is sin; each victory will help you some other to win; fight manfully onward, dark passions subdue; look ever to Jesus – He'll carry you through"* **Palmer**

3. Physical Weakness

During the fast, you may feel weak and tired. This is natural. However, the Holy Spirit – our **helper** and **comforter,** will strengthen you and help you through (John 14:16; Zechariah 4:6).

"I CAN DO all things [which He has called me to do] through Him who STRENGTHENS and EMPOWERS **me** *[to fulfill His purpose—I am self-sufficient in Christ's sufficiency; I am ready for anything and equal to anything* **through Him who** *INFUSES ME with INNER STRENGTH* **and confident peace.***"*

Philippians 4:13 (AMP)

- God will release His supernatural strength into your body.
- The Lord will renew your strength gradually as you progress purposefully.
- You will mount up with wings like eagles.
- You will not be weary. You will not faint (Isaiah 40:29-31).

- The more you feel physical weakness, the stronger and more powerful you are becoming spiritually, hence, the greater the need for you to continue with your fast. This encourages you and urges you on your spiritual journey (Daniel 10:2, 8).
- The purpose of your fast is much more important than any other thing.
- Don't be much concerned about your weight during the fast.
- Keep your eyes fixed on Jesus, focus on the spiritual benefits of your fasting, not on your weight (Hebrews 12:1-4).
- If you are fasting for a Day, 3-Days, 21-Days, 40-Days or for any length of time, let the Lord be glorified in all you do during your fasting.

4. Sleep

Sometimes, you may find it difficult to sleep at night during your fasting due to loss of weight which leaves excess of blood in the body. This may keep you from sleeping a few nights, however, it offers you a good opportunity of prayer and communion with the Lord. This may differ from person to person, though.

5. Dreams, Divine Revelations & Visions

During fasting, the Lord gives us great revelations, dreams and visions about His Kingdom, His plans and purposes for our lives.

The Lord will give you dreams, visions and revelations about your life, your education, career, your marriage relationship, spouse, family, children, your work/job, your church and ministry, your friends, your enemies, your community, your town, city, nation, among other things which relate to you.

Many times, during my fasting, the Lord would reveal a number of things to me about my life, my nuclear family, extended family, my friends and enemies, my ministry and loyal ministry partners, my associate Pastors and church leaders, our missional community, London and the United Kingdom among other things.

There were times that the Lord gave me revelations about some of the great Men and Women of God in the Body of Christ across the globe, which pertain to impartations and passing on of mantles of ministry among other things.

It is very exciting!

These dreams, visions and revelations from God are very encouraging, empowering and helpful in our Christian lives.

It is our Heavenly Father communicating with us in various ways, to provide us with His:

- Fatherly Love and Care
- Divine Guidance
- Divine Direction
- Divine Warning
- Divine Affirmation
- Divine Confirmation
- Divine Acceptance
- Divine Admonition
- Divine Counsel
- Divine Support
- Divine Strength
- Divine Courage
- Divine Provision
- Divine Power
- Divine Instruction
- Divine Favours
- Divine Healing
- Divine Deliverance
- Divine Breakthrough
- Divine Answers
- Divine Connections
- Divine Covering
- Divine Revelations

Key Biblical Examples of Dreams, Divine Revelations & Visions During Biblical Fasting include:

Jesus Christ (Matthew 4:11);
Cornelius (Acts 10:1- 4, 30-33);
Daniel (Daniel 10:1-21, vs. 2-8).

14

23 Reasons Why You Should Fast

1. To Worship, Serve & Minister Unto The LORD

"As they **ministered to the Lord** and **fasted**, the Holy Spirit said, "Now separate to Me Barnabas and Saul for the work to which I have called them." Then, having **fasted and prayed**, and laid hands on them, they sent them away."

Acts 13:2-3 (NKJV)

'Ministered to the Lord' as used in the book of Acts speaks of the disciples' ministry of public *worship* unto God.

"One day as **they were worshiping God**—they were also **fasting as they waited for guidance**—the Holy Spirit spoke: "Take Barnabas and Saul and commission them for the work I have called them to do." So they commissioned them. **In that circle of intensity and obedience, of fasting and praying**, they laid hands on their heads and sent them off."

Acts 13:2-3 (MSG)

We also serve God in prayers and fasting, among other things.

*"While **they were serving the Lord and fasting**, the Holy Spirit said, "Set apart for Me Barnabas and Saul (Paul) for the work to which I have called them." **Then after fasting and praying**, they laid their hands on them [in approval and dedication] and sent them away [on their first journey]."*

Acts 13:2-3 (AMP)

"One day as these men were **worshiping the Lord and fasting,** the Holy Spirit said, "Appoint Barnabas and Saul for the special work to which I have called them." So **after more fasting and prayer**, the men laid their hands on them and sent them on their way."

Acts 13:2-3 (NLT)

During fasting, we minister not unto any man, neither to ourselves, but unto the Lord, then the Lord will *minister* back to us through His Holy Spirit and His Holy angels.

Jesus Christ experienced this when He was on earth:

*"Then **Jesus** was led up by the Spirit into the wilderness... And **when He had fasted forty days and forty nights**, afterward He was hungry."*

Matthew 4:1-2 (NKJV)

*"And He was there in the wilderness **forty days**, tempted of Satan; and was with the wild beasts; **and the angels ministered unto Him**."*

Mark 1:13

2. To Strengthen and Increase Your Faith

*"And the apostles said unto the Lord, **Increase our faith**.*

*And the Lord said, **If ye had faith as a grain of mustard seed**, ye might say unto this sycamine tree, Be thou plucked up by the root, and be thou planted in the sea; and it should obey you."*

Luke 17:5-6

Your faith can be increased. Your faith level can be strengthened. (Mark 11:23-24).

*"Then came the disciples to Jesus apart, and said, Why could not we cast him out? And Jesus said unto them, **Because of your unbelief:** for verily I say unto you, **If ye have faith as a grain of mustard seed**, ye*

shall say unto this mountain, Remove hence to yonder place; and it shall remove; **and nothing shall be impossible unto you."**

Matthew 17:19-20

"Then the disciples came to Jesus privately and asked, "Why could we not drive it out?" He answered, ***"Because of your little faith*** [your lack of trust and confidence in the power of God]; for I assure you and most solemnly say to you, *if you have [living] faith the size of a mustard seed*, you will say to this mountain, 'Move from here to there…and nothing will be impossible for you."

Matthew 17:19-20 (AMP)

The amount of faith you have is not as important as its quality, such small quality Faith can accomplish the humanly impossible.

"Jesus answered and said unto them, Verily I say unto you, ***If ye have faith, and doubt not***, ye shall not only do this which is done to the fig tree, but also if ye shall say unto this mountain, Be thou removed, and be thou cast into the sea; it shall be done.

And all things, whatsoever ye shall ask in prayer, believing, ye shall receive."

Matthew 21:21-22

- Some people have visions of heaven, of glory and of angels during fasting. This greatly increased their Faith. For example, Jesus Christ (Matthew 4:11); Cornelius (Acts 10:1- 4, 30-33); Daniel (Daniel 10:1-21, vs. 2-8).

IMPORTANCE OF FAITH IN PRAYER & FASTING

a. What is Faith?

A Greek root-word for faith is *Pistis*.

The dictionary defines *faith* as complete trust or confidence in someone or something. It is also defined as strong belief in the doctrines of a religion, based on spiritual conviction rather than proof.

Now, let us consider how the Bible defines faith:

"...*faith is the* **substance of things hoped for**, *the evidence of things not seen.*"

Hebrews 11:1

"...*faith is* **the assurance** *(title deed, confirmation)* **of things hoped for (divinely guaranteed)**, *and the evidence of things not seen [the conviction of their reality—faith comprehends as fact what cannot be experienced by the physical senses].*"

Hebrews 11:1 (AMP)

"Faith shows the reality of what we hope for; it is the evidence of things we cannot see."

Hebrews 11:1 (NLT)

Faith means conviction, confidence, trust, believe, reliance, dependence, hope, optimism, expectation and persuasion. Faith is assurance and dependence on God, His covenant promises and all that He says.

It means:

- Believing without evidence.
- To have Confidence in God's power and ability.
- To rely on or depend on God and His word as trustworthy.

b. Why Should We Have Faith?

i. Faith Brings You Healing and Wholeness:

*"Jesus said to her, "Daughter, **you took a risk of faith**, and now **you're healed** and **whole**. Live well, live blessed! Be healed of your plague."*

*"And He said unto her, **Daughter, thy faith hath made thee whole**; go in peace, and be whole of thy plague."*

Mark 5:34

ii. Faith Brings an End to Your Pain and Suffering:

*"And He said to her, "Daughter, **your faith has made you well**. Go in peace. **Your suffering is over.**"*

Mark 5:34 (NLT)

iii. Faith assures us of success, establishment and security in life:

*"...**Believe** in the Lord your God, so shall **ye be established**..."*

2 Chronicles 20:20

*"...Believe and **trust in the Lord** your God and **you will be** established (secure)..."*

2 Chronicles 20:20 (AMP)

iv. Faith is an indispensable element in our walk with God as Christians.

Without faith, it is impossible to please God:

*"But **without faith it is impossible to [walk with God and] please Him,** for whoever comes [near] to God must [necessarily] believe that God exists..."*

Hebrews 11:6 (AMP)

It is the fundamental duty of a believer to have faith in God.

*"But **without faith it is impossible to please Him**: for he that cometh to God must believe that He is..."*

Hebrews 11:6

*"And **it is impossible to please God without faith**. Anyone who wants to come to Him must believe that God exists..."*

Hebrews 11:6 (NLT)

v. **Faith will sustain you through the challenges,** through the fires, and the floods of life. It worked for Shadrach, Meshach and Abednego, so it will work for you (Daniel 3:17-25; John 6:28-29).

vi. **Faith is a defensive armor for spiritual warfare,** for winning life's battles and for overcoming the enemy:

*"Above all, **taking the shield of faith**, wherewith ye shall be able **to quench all the fiery darts of the wicked.**"*

Ephesians 6:16

*"Above all, lift up **the [protective] shield of faith** with which you can **extinguish all the flaming arrows of the evil one.**"*

Ephesians 6:16 (AMP)

*"In addition to all of these, **hold up the shield of faith to stop the fiery arrows of the devil.**"*

Ephesians 6:16 (NLT)

vii. **We are justified by Faith:**

"Therefore being justified by faith, we have peace with God..."

Romans 5:1

"Therefore, since we have been **made right in God's sight by faith**, we have peace with God..."

Romans 5:1 (NLT)

"Therefore, since we have been **justified [that is, acquitted of sin, declared blameless before God] by faith,** [let us grasp the fact that] we have peace with God [and the joy of reconciliation with Him]..."

Romans 5:1 (AMP)

viii. **We are Saved by God's Grace through Our Faith:**

"For by **grace** are ye **saved** through **faith**..."

Ephesians 2:8-9

"**God saved** you by **His grace** when **you believed**..."

Ephesians 2:8-9 (NLT)

"For **it is by grace** [God's remarkable compassion and favour drawing you to Christ] that **you have been saved** [actually delivered from judgment **and given eternal life] through faith**..."

Ephesians 2:8-9 (AMP)

ix. Faith is an Essential Element of Prayer

*"If any of you lack wisdom, let him ask of God...**But let him ask in faith**, nothing wavering. For he that wavereth is like a wave of the sea driven with the wind and tossed. For **let not that man think that he shall receive any thing of the Lord**. A double minded man is unstable in all his ways."*

James 1:5-8

x. Faith Casts Out Demons of All Kinds

'...a man came up to Jesus, kneeling before Him and saying, "Lord, have mercy on my son, for he is a lunatic (moonstruck) and suffers terribly; for he often falls into the fire and often into the water. And *I brought him to Your disciples, and they were not able to heal him."* And Jesus answered, *"You unbelieving* and perverted generation...Bring him here to Me." **Jesus rebuked the demon, and it came out of him, and the boy was healed at once.**

Then the disciples came to Jesus privately and asked, **"Why could we not drive it out?"** He answered, *"BECAUSE OF YOUR LITTLE FAITH* [your lack of trust and confidence in the power of God]; for I assure you and most solemnly say to you, *if you have [living] faith the size of a mustard seed, you will say to this mountain, 'Move from here to there,'* and...it will move; and nothing will be impossible for you. *But THIS KIND OF DEMON DOES NOT GO OUT EXCEPT BY PRAYER AND FASTING.]"*

Matthew 17:14-21 (AMP)

TYPES OF FAITH

i. No Faith

There are people who have no faith at all. Faith develops in you as you begin to believe in God, hear His Word and Obey His Word.

Jesus *said to them, "Why are you afraid?* ***Do you still have NO FAITH*** *and confidence [in Me]?"*

Mark 4:40 (AMP)

Jesus *reprimanded the disciples: "Why are you such cowards?* ***DON'T YOU HAVE ANY FAITH AT ALL?"***

Mark 4:40 (MSG)

*"And He said unto them, Why are ye so fearful? How is it that ye have **NO FAITH**?"*

Mark 4:40

ii. Weak Faith

Abraham was commended as a Servant of God who was not weak in faith. Weak faith is that which wavers, is unstable, doubtful, uncertain, and often leads to double-mindedness.

"And being not **WEAK IN FAITH**, he considered not his own body now dead, when he was about an hundred years old, neither yet the deadness of Sarah's womb"

Romans 4:19

"Without becoming **weak in faith** he considered his own body, now as good as dead [for producing children] since he was about a hundred years old, and [he considered] the deadness of Sarah's womb."

Romans 4:19 (AMP)

"And Abraham's **FAITH did not WEAKEN**, even though, at about 100 years of age, he figured his body was as good as dead—and so was Sarah's womb."

Romans 4:19 (NLT)

xviii. Little Faith

Little faith is Under-Developed Faith. Jesus exhorts the disciples on Under-Developed Faith in the gospel of Matthew:

"Wherefore, if God so clothe the grass of the field, which today is, and tomorrow is cast into the oven, shall he not much more clothe you, **O ye of LITTLE FAITH?**"

Matthew 6:30

"And if God cares so wonderfully for wildflowers that are here today and thrown into the fire tomorrow, he will certainly care for you. **Why do you have so LITTLE FAITH?**"

Matthew 6:30 (NLT)

"It is God who clothes the wild grass—grass that is here today and gone tomorrow, burned up in the oven. Won't he be all the more sure to clothe you? **What LITTLE FAITH you have!**"

Matthew 6:30 (GNT)

We Need Faith to Overcome and Override the Storms of Life:

"When He got into the boat, His disciples followed Him. And suddenly a violent storm arose on the sea, so that the boat was being covered by the waves; but Jesus was sleeping. And the disciples went and woke Him, saying, "Lord, save us, we are going to die!" *He said to them, "Why are you afraid,* **you men of LITTLE FAITH?**" *Then He got up and rebuked the winds and the sea, and there was [at once] a great and wonderful calm [a perfect peacefulness].* The men wondered in amazement, saying, "What kind of man is this, that even the winds and the sea obey Him?"

Matthew 8:23-27 (AMP)

xix. Strong Faith

The Bible described **Abraham** as a man of strong faith, for:

*"… he considered not his own body now dead, when he was about an hundred years old, neither yet the deadness of Sarah's womb: He staggered not at the promise of God through unbelief; but was **STRONG IN FAITH**, giving glory to God"*

Romans 4:19-20

*"Abraham never wavered in believing God's promise. In fact, **his FAITH GREW STRONGER,** and in this he brought glory to God."*

Romans 4:20 (NLT)

xx. Great Faith

"Now when Jesus had entered Capernaum, a centurion came to Him, pleading with Him, saying, "Lord, my servant is lying at home paralyzed, dreadfully tormented."

And Jesus said to him, "I will come and heal him."

The centurion answered and said, "Lord, I am not worthy that You should come under my roof. But only speak a word, and my servant will be healed. For I also am a man under authority, having soldiers under me. And I say to this *one*, 'Go,' and he goes; and to another, 'Come,' and he comes; and to my servant, 'Do this,' and he does it."

When Jesus heard *it*, He marveled, and said to those who followed, *"Assuredly, I say to you,* ***I have not found such GREAT FAITH****, not even in Israel!"*

Matthew 8:5-10 (NKJV)

xxi.   Stubborn Faith

The faith exhibited by the 3 Servants of the Most High God, Shadrach, Meshach and Abednego in Babylon in the presence of King Nebuchadnezzar and all the people of the land is what I call stubborn faith (Daniel 3:11-30).

By virtue of their faith, listen to what they said:

"Shadrach, Meshach, and Abednego, answered and said to the king, O Nebuchadnezzar, we are not careful to answer thee in this matter.

If it be so, ***our God whom we serve is able to deliver us from the burning fiery furnace, and He will deliver us out of thine hand****, O king.*

But if not, be it known unto thee, O king, that we will not serve thy gods, nor worship the golden image *which thou hast set up."*

Daniel 3:16-18

> **PowerPoint:**
>
> *Your Faith will release Heavenly Power and Earthly Blessings and Rewards to you.*

Strengthen Your Faith Through The Fasting-Prayer

And the apostles said to the Lord, *"Increase our faith"* **(Luke 17:5-6)**.

Our faith grows and increases as we feed on the word of God. The amount of faith you have is not as important as its spiritual wave-length in quality. Such small quality faith can accomplish the humanly impossible for the benefit of humanity and to the glory of God. Some people have visions of heaven, of eternal glory, of future events, and of angels during fasting; these greatly increase their faith.

Examples include **Jesus Christ** (Matthew 4:11,);

Cornelius (Acts 10:1-4, 30-33); **Daniel** (Daniel 10:1-21).

> **PowerPoint:**
>
> *Fasting brings Heart-Faith to believe in the words and promises of God.*

Many Christians genuinely believe, but the fact remains that there is a *"Heart-Faith"* that 'provokes' and releases miracles from the Lord (Mark 11:23-24). The closer we draw to God in prayer and the Word, the more we are able to believe His covenant promises and receive miracles from Him.

The Scriptures say,

*"For **with the heart man believeth** unto righteousness; and with the mouth confession is made unto salvation."*

Romans 10:10

*"Jesus said to him, "**If you can believe**, all things are possible to **him who believes**."*

Mark 9:23 (NKJV)

To Him who believes, all things are possible. If you have faith, nothing shall be impossible to you.

- Fasting-prayer ignites your faith to pray and lay hands on the sick to be healed and delivered from demonic oppression and influence, including your own sicknesses.

- Fasting-prayer releases faith that causes troublesome, difficult, unsaved, impatient, and rebellious spouses to be brought to Christ, transformed and changed for good.

- Fasting-prayer releases faith that causes broken homes to be repaired, renewed, revived and reunited.
- Fating-prayer releases faith to see mountains of problems and challenges of life moved (Matthew 17:20).

3. For Spiritual Empowerment

*"And Jesus being **full of the Holy Ghost** returned from Jordan, and was **led by the Spirit** into the wilderness, And **Jesus returned in the power of the Spirit** into Galilee: and there went out a fame of Him through all the region round about. And he taught in their synagogues, being glorified of all."*

(Luke 4:1, 14-15)

The Christian life is one of warfare.

The Scripture says;

*"For **we wrestle** not against flesh and blood, but **against principalities, against powers, against the rulers of the darkness of this world,** against **spiritual wickedness** in high places."*

Ephesians 6:12

There is the need, however, for every believer to remain constantly empowered, armed and filled with the Spirit of God to overcome sin, temptation and the forces of darkness. You also need divine empowerment to fulfill your God-given dreams, vision, aspirations, hopes and purpose on earth.

After 3 days of employing the fasting-prayer, Queen Esther was empowered by the Spirit of God to strategically make wise moves and take destiny steps of victory for herself and the Jews.

You need Spiritual empowerment for victorious Christian living by engaging the fasting-prayer. God will open doors of blessings for you because you are focused on servicing God's Kingdom Advancement Programmes. Jesus fasted and prayed in the wilderness for spiritual empowerment and preparation to fulfill His purpose and mission on earth.

Fasting may render us physically empty and ready to be re-filled, energized, empowered and renewed afresh and anew by the Holy Spirit and the unlimited power of the miracle working-God. God also releases spiritual gifts to us during this time of waiting on Him. Fasting that is devoid of Bible reading, Bible study, meditation in the word of God and prayer, leaves a person at the 'mercy and manipulation of evil spirits and demonic powers. This is very dangerous. Be vigilant, beware, be awake and spend quality time in the word of God.

4. To Give Ourselves Devotedly To Prayer

*"Defraud ye not one the other, except it be with consent for a time, **that ye may GIVE YOURSELVES to FASTING and PRAYER...**"*

1 Corinthians 7:5

Fasting time is a time to really pray to God. The Bible exhorts us to pray. Prayer is one of the believer's powerful tools, a weapon for warfare, a potent key that opens every door for solutions and answers to life's issues and challenges.

*"Do not deprive each other [of marital rights], except perhaps by mutual consent for a time, **so that you may DEVOTE YOURSELVES [unhindered] to PRAYER...**"*

1 Corinthians 7:5 (AMP)

*"Marriage is not a place to "stand up for your rights." Marriage is a decision to serve the other, whether in bed or out. Abstaining from sex is permissible for a period of time if you both agree to it, and if it's **for the purposes of prayer and fasting**—but only for such times..."*

1 Corinthians 7:5-6 (MSG)

*"Do not deprive each other of sexual relations, unless you both agree to refrain from sexual intimacy for a limited time **so you can GIVE YOURSELVES more COMPLETELY to PRAYER...**"*

1 Corinthians 7:5 (NLT)

"This is why the twelve Apostles of Jesus called the multitude of the disciples in the early church and said;

"...WE WILL GIVE OURSELVES **continually to PRAYER...**"

Acts 6:2, 4

Prayer moves the hand of God to act on our behalf and for kingdom expansion.

"*For from days of old no one has heard, nor has ear perceived, Nor has the eye seen* **a God besides You, Who WORKS and ACTS in BEHALF of the one who [gladly] WAITS for Him.**"

Isaiah 64:4 (AMP)

"*For since the world began, no ear has heard and no eye has seen* **a God like You, Who WORKS for THOSE who WAIT for HIM!**"

Isaiah 64:4 (NLT)

Fasting sharpens prayer, therefore, fasting time is prayer time. Even in marriage, Christian couples may have their sexual activities 'interrupted' based on 3 main necessary conditions, biblically advised, one being prayer and fasting;

1. Mutual consent (1 Corinthians 7:5).
2. A limited time (1 Corinthians 7:5).

3. Spiritual reasons – prayer and fasting, not for selfish reasons (1 Cor. 7:5).

It is helpful when couples set aside some time to fast and pray for our marriage, children, family, home, and our local churches, ministers and ministries. The devil is at war against Christian marriages, Christian homes and Christian families, however, we should not be unaware of the devices of the enemy. As we fast and supplicate together, we will joyfully experience the God-ordained blessings, favours and peace in our marriages and in our homes. The fasting-prayer should not only be employed during courtship or before marriage, but, equally during the lifetime of the marriage.

5. To Mortify the Flesh and Walk in the Spirit

The Scripture says;

*"**Mortify** therefore **your members** which are upon the earth; fornication, uncleanness, inordinate affection, evil concupiscence, and covetousness, which is idolatry"*

Colossians 3:5

"So **put to death** and **deprive of power the evil longings of your earthly body** [with its sensual, self-centered instincts] immorality, impurity, sinful passion, evil desire, and greed, which is [a kind of] idolatry [because it replaces your devotion to God]."

Colossians 3:5 (AMP)

"And that means killing off everything connected with that way of death: sexual promiscuity, impurity, lust, doing whatever you feel like whenever you feel like it, and grabbing whatever attracts your fancy. That's a life shaped by things and feelings instead of by God. It's because of this kind of thing that God is about to explode in anger. It wasn't long ago that you were doing all that stuff and not knowing any better. But you know better now, so make sure it's all gone for good: bad temper, irritability, meanness, profanity, dirty talk."

Colossians 3:5 (MSG)

*"So **put to death the sinful, earthly things lurking within you**. Have nothing to do with sexual immorality, impurity, lust, and evil desires. Don't be greedy, for a greedy person is an idolater, worshiping the things of this world."*

Colossians 3:5 (NLT)

The fasting-prayer enables and empowers us to come out of, step out of, switch from the natural, and connect with the *supernatural*; from the *ordinary* into the *extra-ordinary*.

According to Scripture, there is always war, battle, conflict between the spirit and the flesh; between our natural desires and the Spirit of the Lord (Holy Spirit) in the life of the believer. One of the two always wins, depending on where we tilt to, which voice we listen to [the voice of God, the devil or our flesh], whom we obey [God or Satan], and the choices and decisions that we make from day to day.

Walk in the Spirit

The bible says "**Walk in the Spirit, and you shall not fulfill the lust of the flesh**. For the flesh lusts against the Spirit, and the Spirit against the flesh; and these are contrary to one another, so that you do not do the things that you wish. But if you are led by the Spirit, you are not under the law.

Now **the works of the flesh are evident**, which are: adultery, fornication, uncleanness, lewdness, idolatry, sorcery, hatred, contentions, jealousies, outbursts of wrath, selfish ambitions, dissensions, heresies, envy, murders, drunkenness, revelries, and the like;…those who practice such things will not inherit the kingdom of God.

But the fruit of the Spirit is love, joy, peace, longsuffering, kindness, goodness, faithfulness, gentleness, self-control…And THOSE WHO ARE CHRIST'S HAVE CRUCIFIED THE FLESH WITH ITS PASSIONS AND DESIRES. If we live in the Spirit, let us also walk in the Spirit. Let us not become conceited, provoking one another, envying one another."

Galatians 5:16-26 (NKJV)

Fasting for about 3 days, a week, 2 or 3 weeks will help you discover how much of your *"Old Man"* (**sinful desires**) still need to be crucified. Jesus went through this (40 days and nights) when He walked on this earth more than 2 thousand years ago, and He dealt with the *flesh and its desires*.

During fasting, our weaknesses, secret sins and fleshly desires are more clearly revealed as we tune to the Holy Spirit. The Holy Spirit then empowers and enables us to mortify them by crucifying them to the cross of Christ, so as to completely surrender our hearts and yield our will to the will of God. The Holy Spirit then fills us and uses our lives to touch other people's lives to the glory of God, and to serve God in other various ways for the expansion of His Kingdom.

6. To Release Souls to Populate Heaven by Faith & To Pray the Lord of the Harvest to Send Labourers into His Harvest

It is sad, unreasonable and impossible to say that we are following Jesus if we are not concerned about those who are not saved, and if we do not make any effort to reach the unreached with the Gospel of the Kingdom and win souls for Christ.

The Bible says,

"The LORD is…NOT WILLING that ANY should PERISH, but that ALL should come to REPENTANCE."

2 Peter 3:9

"God…doesn't want ANYONE LOST. He's giving EVERYONE space and time TO CHANGE."

2 Peter 3:9 (MSG)

"The LORD…does not want anyone to be destroyed, but WANTS EVERYONE TO REPENT."

2 Peter 3:9 (NLT)

God is not willing that anyone should perish, but that all people everywhere should hear the gospel, that, God loves them and Jesus died on the cross of Calvary for the forgiveness of their sins, the salvation of their souls, and made a provision for them to spend eternity with God when they leave this earth. All people, everywhere in the world need to be saved from sin.

This is why the Bible says,

"I exhort therefore, that, first of all, SUPPLICATIONS, PRAYERS, INTERCESSIONS, and giving of thanks, BE MADE FOR ALL…"

1 Timothy 2:1

This is where our fasting-prayer is most effective and relevant in praying for the repentance of all people and the Holy Spirit will convict their hearts and prepare them to respond to the gospel of Jesus Christ.

The Scripture says,

"SAVE others, SNATCHING THEM OUT OF THE FIRE; and on some, have mercy but with fear, loathing even the clothing spotted and polluted by their shameless immoral freedom."

Jude 1:23 (AMP)

"RESCUE OTHERS by snatching them FROM THE FLAMES OF JUDGMENT. Show mercy to...others, but do so with great caution, hating the sins that contaminate their lives."

Jude 1:23 (NLT)

- Every child of God is under heavenly obligation to be a Soul Winner.
- God will use our fasting-prayers to prepare people's hearts to receive the gospel, to believe in, and receive Jesus Christ as their personal Lord and Saviour.
- Our prayers will win souls for Christ.
- Our evangelism and community outreach efforts will bring souls to Christ.
- Our preaching and teaching of the Word of God will bring souls to Christ.
- Our Christ-like living and Godly conduct will bring souls to Christ.

- Our sincere love for one another as Brothers and Sisters in Christ will bring souls to Christ.

"Then Jesus said…***Follow Me, and I will make you become fishers of men***."

Mark 1:17 (NKJV)

"And Jesus said…**Follow Me [as My disciples**, accepting Me as your Master and Teacher and walking the same path of life that I walk], and **I will make you fishers of men.**"

Mark 1:17 (AMP)

"Jesus called out…Come, *follow me,* and *I will show you* how *to fish for people!*"

Mark 1:17 (NLT)

Biblical Fasting must be accompanied by an intense heart desire to see the lost, the unsaved and sinners brought from darkness into light. Jesus is the light of the world (John 8:12).

- Jesus has saved us and asked us to follow Him so we can bring others to His glorious Kingdom.

The Almighty God says,

"**Ask of Me,** and **I will** assuredly **give [You] the nations** as Your inheritance, And **the ends of the earth** as Your possession."

Psalm 2:8 (AMP)

- The unreached people, communities, villages, cities, towns and nations are ours for the asking by employing the Fasting-prayer.
- Jesus publicly made a request for labourers who will pray-in and reach-out to the harvest-field and bring lost souls into the Kingdom of God.

He said,

"...**The harvest** is abundant **[for there are many who need to hear the good news about salvation]**, but the workers **[those available to proclaim the message of salvation] are few**. Therefore, [PRAYERFULLY] ASK the LORD of the HARVEST TO SEND OUT WORKERS into His harvest."

Luke 10:12 (AMP)

These call for employing the fasting-prayer, because of:

1. The deliverance and translation of lost souls from the kingdom of darkness (**Colossians 1:13**).

2. The need to take them by force - the force of intense spiritual warfare (**Matthew 11:12**).
3. The need to bind the strong man [the devil and forces of darkness] who are leading souls down the broad way to hell (**Matthew 12:29; Matthew 18:18**).

> "...***The harvest truly is great***, *but the labourers are few:* ***PRAY YE…the LORD of the harvest***, *that He would send forth labourers into His harvest."*
>
> **Luke 10:12**

Many of us Christians sadly rejoice with the level of our Christian lives without making time for the Heartbeat of God - (unsaved souls).

- Such Christians are compared to the fruitless fig-tree which Jesus cursed for not bearing fruit (Matthew 21:18-12).
- We must bear the fruit of Love by winning the lost for Christ.

The fasting prayer is able to set you free from the chains of laziness, ignorance, lack of Godly-vision and Kingdom-Passion and Spiritual-fervency which enables you to get occupied with the things of God and be busy with God's Kingdom Business (GKB).

- If you're not able to preach in the pulpit in your local church, you can visit the hospitals and engage with hospital ministry.
- Reach out to the prisons and engage with prison ministry.
- Go on the streets, the highways, byways, broad ways, bus-stops, train/tram/tube stations (Matthew 7:13).

Unsaved Souls are everywhere, waiting for someone to share the gospel of Christ with them. You are that vessel that God wants to use to reach out to some of them. Are you ready?

Hospital and Prison Ministries

Are you too busy to serve the Lord?

There was a certain University Senior Lecturer who is an elderly man, he is a good and Godly husband and faithful father in his home, a committed church worker and leader, a Full Gospel Business Men's Fellowship Ex-President and Executive, among other things. This precious senior citizen and brother in the Lord has every human excuse to keep out of the Kingdom harvest, however, for his love for the Lord and for God's Kingdom Business, brother Felix Ameku made time 2 days every week to reach out to the prisoners at the Winneba prisons and the patients at the Winneba government hospital in Ghana, Africa, with the gospel and prayer time. Brother Felix has a great passion for the harvest of lost souls. He was a very active church worker in the Assemblies of God church, and a very diligent senior University lecturer, however, none of those commitments prevented him from fulfilling His God-given assignments for the Kingdom of God every week of his life.

- My dear young man, young woman, how busy are you for God?
- How are you spending your life, your time, your energy and your resources every day?

This is the time to invest your life, your time and your resources in the things of God, for eternal rewards when your life on this earth comes to an end.

Employ the fasting-prayer for unsaved souls in your family, your neighbourhood and community, your school/college/university/place of work, and in your country.

7. **Certain Problems and Challenges of Life Cannot Be Solved Except by Prayer and Fasting.**

Jesus said,

*"However, THIS KIND DOES NOT GO OUT **except by PRAYER and FASTING.**"*

Matthew 17:21 (NKJV)

*"But THIS KIND OF DEMON does not go out **except by prayer and fasting.**"*

Matthew 17:21 (AMP)

Some areas of victory in your life will never be realized except through fasting and prayer. Examine your life and plan a fast. God will grant you victory.

Certain evil spirits and demons cannot be bound and cast out unless you employ the fasting-prayer. As you fast and pray, bind and cast out all unclean spirits that influence your life and family and they will loose their hold over your life and family.

Jesus Has Given Us Power Over All Demonic Forces & Evil Spirits

*"And when He had called unto Him His twelve disciples, **He gave them** POWER AGAINST UNCLEAN SPIRITS, to CAST THEM OUT, and to heal all manner of sickness and all manner of disease."*

Matthew 10:1

"Jesus summoned His twelve disciples and **gave them AUTHORITY and POWER OVER UNCLEAN SPIRITS, to CAST THEM OUT,** and to heal every kind of disease and every kind of sickness."

Matthew 10:1 (AMP)

"**Submit yourselves** therefore **to God. RESIST THE DEVIL,** and he **WILL FLEE** from you."

James 4:7

*"So **submit to** [the authority of] **God. RESIST the DEVIL [stand firm against him] and he WILL FLEE from you.**"*

James 4:7 (AMP)

"So **humble** yourselves **before God. RESIST** the **DEVIL,** and **he will FLEE from you.**"

James 4:7 (NLT)

*"So let God work His will in you. **YELL a LOUD NO to the Devil** and watch him scamper."*

James 4:7 (MSG)

- Certain marriage-relationships cannot be contracted or entered into, except by employing the fasting-prayer.

"*The **effectual fervent** PRAYER of a righteous man availeth much.*"

James 5:16b

"The **heartfelt** and **persistent** PRAYER of a righteous man (believer) **can accomplish much** [when put into action and made effective by God—it is dynamic and **can have tremendous power**]."

James 5:16b (AMP)

- Certain marriages cannot thrive fruitfully according to God's kingdom plan and purpose, but by prayer and fasting. (Family curses must be broken and family spirits dealt with appropriately by the fasting-prayer). Hannah, who could not have children, employed the fasting-prayer, God opened her womb, and she became the mother of Samuel, the Prophet of Israel and 6 other children (1 Samuel 1:1-28; 1 Samuel 2:1-5).

Hannah prayed and said,

*"My heart rejoices and triumphs in the Lord; My horn (strength) is lifted up in the Lord, My mouth has opened wide [to speak boldly]... **Even the barren [woman] gives birth to seven.**"*

1 Samuel 2:1, 5c (AMP)

- Certain businesses and ministries cannot breakthrough obstacles and experience expansion and enlargement without prayer and fasting.

Moses, the man of God, Prayed;

"And let the beauty of the Lord our God be upon us, And **establish the work of our hands** for us; Yes, **establish the work of our hands**."

Psalm 90:17 (NKJV)

"And may the Lord our God show us his approval and **make our efforts successful**. Yes, **make our efforts successful**!"

Psalm 90:17 (NLT)

- During your fasting, confess your sins to God, ask Him to remove all obstacles to your progress and success, and to establish, expand and enlarge your work, your business, your ministry, your career.

- Some people may not experience healing from certain demonically influenced chronic sicknesses, diseases and infirmities without employing the fasting-prayer.

Jesus Christ clearly emphasized this point in **Matthew 17:14-21**. By virtue of Jesus' fasting and prayer-life, backed by His authority, the little boy who was epileptic, lunatic (moonstruck) and suffers terribly; and often falls into the fire and often into the water, was healed of his infirmity as Jesus rebuked and cast out the evil spirit which was behind that health condition.

PRAYER: *In the mighty name of Jesus, I rebuke every evil spirit influencing any condition, situation and circumstance in my life, marriage relationship, family and my destiny by the power of the Holy Spirit, Amen!*

Please personalize the above prayer in every concerned area of your life, family and ministry – spiritually, physically and financially.

- Some rebellious, troublesome, difficult and prodigal children cannot be brought back Home soundly without prayer and fasting.

During my early years, I was living with my grandmother from whom my journey to faith in Christ started. Dada Monica was a very devout and prayerful woman of God. I remember how fervently she used to pray every night for one prodigal grandson called Jonathan, who fled to Abidjan, Côte d'Ivoire with some of her treasures. After a season, God answered her prayers and Jonathan returned, but not in good shape. I saw how countless prayers of my grandmother graciously received answers from God. By the special grace of God, for me to be serving the Lord and fulfilling the call of God at this level in my humble life is partly one of the answers to heartfelt prayers of my grandmother for her grandchildren.

Prayer works!

God answers Prayer!

Keep your Prayer Fires Burning.

- Some peculiar problems may not be solved, but by prayer and fasting (Esther 4:12-17)

- Bible study assignment – Please study the book of Esther and relate the story prayerfully). Be blessed!

8. For Right Directions, Divine Intervention, Wise and Godly Decisions in Our Lives, Families, Ministries and Nations.

a. Queen Esther said to Modecai,

"Go, gather together all the Jews that are present in Shushan, and *fast* ye for me, and **neither eat nor drink three days, night or day:** I also and **my maidens** will **fast** likewise; and SO WILL I GO IN UNTO THE KING, which is not according to the law: and if I perish, I perish."

Esther 4:16

b. Ezra said,

"Then I proclaimed *a fast* there at the river of Ahava, **that we might humble ourselves before**

our God, TO SEEK FROM HIM THE RIGHT WAY *for us and our little ones and all our possessions.* For I was ashamed to request of the king an escort of soldiers and horsemen to help us against the enemy on the road, because we had spoken to the king, saying, "The hand of our God is upon all those for good who seek Him, but His power and His wrath *are* against all those who forsake Him." So we *fasted and entreated our God for this, and He answered our prayer.*

Ezra 8:21-23 (NKJV)

9. **To Be Filled With the Holy Spirit and Manifest His Fruit and Gifts.** (Galatians 5:22-23; I Corinthians 12:1-31; Mark 16:17-18)

Prayer and fasting opens doors for supernatural manifestations of the Holy Spirit to flow in abundance. A purposeful life of fasting and prayer in the Spirit rekindles the flame of the gifts and power of the Holy Spirit in us and keeps it burning.

"But you, beloved, **build yourselves up** *on [the foundation of] your most holy faith [continually progress,* **rise** *like an edifice* **higher and higher], PRAY in the Holy Spirit.***"*

Jude 20 (AMP)

A praying and fasting believer who is continually sober, serious and thoughtful; solemn and watchful in the spirit has the advantage of keeping himself from falling.

"...brethren, **give diligence** to make your calling and election sure: for ***if ye do these things, ye shall never fall.***"

2 Peter 1:10

"Therefore, believers, be all the more diligent to make certain about His calling and choosing you [be sure that your behaviour reflects and confirms your relationship with God]; for by doing these things **[*actively developing these virtues*], you will never stumble [in your spiritual growth** and will live a life that leads others away from sin]"

2 Peter 1:10 (AMP)

"So, dear brothers and sisters, **work hard to prove** that you really are among those God has called and chosen. Do these things, and *you will never fall away.*"

2 Peter 1:10 (NLT)

Fasting and prayer will help stir up the gifts of God in your life for effective Christian living and for fulfilling your ministry and the call of God upon your life. (II Tim. 1:6)

"...**stir up** the **gift of God**, which is **in thee**..."

2 Timothy 1:6

"...**fan into flames** the **spiritual gift God** gave you..."

2 Timothy 1:6 (NLT)

"...**fan into flame** the gracious **gift of God**, [that *inner fire—the special endowment*] which is in you..."

2 Timothy 1:6 (AMP)

"...the **special gift of ministry** you received...—**keep that ablaze!**"

2 Timothy 1:6 (MSG)

10. To Humble Ourselves Before God and Under His Mighty Hand

Pastor Ezra said,

*"Then **I proclaimed a fast** there...that we might **HUMBLE OURSELVE** before our God..."*

Ezra 8:21 (NKJV)

Humbling ourselves before God and under His mighty hand releases more of God's Grace, lifting, exaltation and promotion upon our lives.

"**HUMBLE** yourselves therefore **under** *the mighty hand of God*, that **He may EXALT YOU** in due time"

1 Peter 5:6

"Therefore HUMBLE yourselves *under the mighty hand of God [set aside self-righteous pride]*, so that **He may** EXALT YOU [to a place of HONOUR **in His service**] at the appropriate time"

1 Peter 5:6 (AMP)

"So HUMBLE yourselves under the mighty power of God, and at the right time **He will** LIFT YOU UP IN HONOUR."

1 Peter 5:6 (NLT)

When we go before God in fasting with a heart of humility, demonstrating our faith and dependence on God, the covenant blessings of the Lord promised in 2 Chronicles 7:14 will be released and fulfilled in our lives, families and ministries.

The Lord says,

"If My people who are called by My name will **humble themselves, and pray and seek My face, and turn from their wicked ways,** then I WILL HEAR FROM HEAVEN, and will FORGIVE THEIR SIN and HEAL THEIR LAND."

2 Chronicles 7:14

This draws God's attention onto you for promotion, exaltation, healing and restoration.

11. **To Intercede for the Sick and Afflicted.**

King David fasted and interceded for the baby of Bathsheba.

"And the Lord struck the child that Uriah's widow bore to David, and he was very sick. David therefore appealed to God for the child [to be healed]; and David fasted and went in and lay all night on the ground. The elders of his household stood by him [in the night] to lift him up from the ground, but he was unwilling [to get up] and would not eat food with them."

Samuel 12:15-17

12. **To Discover and Know God's Plan, Mission and Vision for Our Lives, Families, Ministries, Churches and Nations.**

a. *The Antioch church:*

"Now in the church at Antioch…While **they were serving the Lord and fasting,** the **Holy Spirit said, "Set apart for Me Barnabas and Saul (Paul) for the work to which I have called them."** Then after **fasting and praying**, they laid their hands on them [in approval and dedication] and sent them away [on their first journey]."

Acts 13:1-3 (AMP)

(i). GOD'S PLAN ⟶ To set apart Barnabas & Saul
(ii). MISSION ⟶ For the Work of Ministry
(iii). VISION ⟶ God's Vision for calling them

Note:

- God spoke to the leadership of the Antioch Church (Acts 13:2).

- Preparation of Barnabas and Saul, recognition and acceptance of their calling and ministry (Acts 13:2).

- Corporate prayer and fasting, laying on of hands by the Church as an Act of spiritual impartation and commissioning (Acts 13:3).

b. *Pastor Ezra and the exiled Jews*

"I **proclaimed a fast** there beside the Ahava Canal, **a fast** to humble ourselves **before our God** and PRAY FOR WISE GUIDANCE for our journey—all OUR PEOPLE and POSSESSIONS. I was embarrassed to ask the king for a cavalry bodyguard to PROTECT US from bandits on the road. We had just told the king, "**Our God lovingly looks after all those who seek him**, but turns away in disgust from those who leave Him."

Ezra 8:21

Let's consider the **three-fold purpose** of Ezra's national fast:

i. **GUIDANCE:** To seek from God a "RIGHT WAY" for their lives *(Ezra 8:21)*.

ii. **PETITION for PROTECTION:** for their little ones [children] *(Ezra 8:21)*.

iii. **God to GUARD their POSSESSIONS** *(Ezra 8:21)*.

13. To Receive Destiny-shaping Information from the Lord.

- During Moses' 40 days fast, he received destiny shaping information directly from God for himself, his ministry and the people under his Pastoral care, which otherwise he couldn't receive **(Exodus 34:28-30)**.

- Daniel employed the fasting-prayer for 21-days and a heavenly messenger was sent with a message from God in answer to Daniel's prayer **(Daniel 10:1-21)**.

In the case of Daniel, God sent an angel to release that divine information of Liberty to him. The Prince of Persia withstood the heavenly messenger for 21 days, and God sent angel Michael, one of the Chief Princes in heaven to help him. As you spend quality time in God's holy presence praying, God will speak to you so divinely from heaven and reveal great destiny-shaping mysteries to you.

14. **To Receive Covenant Blessings and Rewards from the Lord.**

Jesus mentioned this in His teaching on fasting. He said,

"…when **you fast**, do not be like the hypocrites, with a sad countenance. For they disfigure their faces that they may appear to men to be **fasting**. Assuredly, I say to you, they have their reward. **But you**, when **you fast**, anoint your head and wash your face, *so that you do not appear to men to be fasting*, but *to your FATHER who is in the secret place; and* YOUR FATHER WHO SEES in SECRET WILL REWARD YOU OPENLY"

Matthew 6:16-18 (NKJV)

"so that **your fasting** will not be noticed by people, but by your Father who is in secret; and **YOUR FATHER who sees [what is done] in secret WILL REWARD YOU.**"

Matthew 6:18 (AMP)

"Then no one will notice that you are fasting, except your Father, who knows what you do in private. And your Father, who sees everything, **will reward you.**"

Matthew 6:18 (NLT)

15. To Plead the Cause of Our Communities, Cities, Nations, and for God's Intervention to Preserve Life, Maintain Peace and Progress

God Almighty sent Jonah to proclaim a message of repentance, judgment and destruction [which was to take place in 40 days] against Nineveh for their wickedness and sin.

The great city of Nineveh proclaimed a fast, when they heard the God-sent message of "Repentance and Mercy" through the prophet Jonah. Human beings and animals fasted, they cried mightily to the God of heaven for the forgiveness of their sins and the sins of the entire city, they repented, turned from their evil ways and God preserved their lives and the entire city.

"The people of Nineveh believed and trusted in God; and they proclaimed a fast and put on sackcloth [in penitent mourning], from the greatest even to the least of them. When word reached the king of Nineveh [of Jonah's message from God], he rose from his throne, took off his robe, covered himself with sackcloth and sat in the dust [in repentance]. He issued a proclamation and it said, "In Nineveh, by the decree of the king and his nobles: No man, animal, herd, or flock is to taste anything. They are not to eat or drink water. But both man and animal must be covered with sackcloth; and everyone is to call on God earnestly and forcefully that each may turn from his wicked way and from the violence that is in his hands. Who knows, God may turn [in compassion] and relent and withdraw His burning anger (judgment) so that we will not perish."

When *God saw their deeds, that they turned from their wicked way,* then **God [had compassion and] relented concerning the disaster which He had declared that He would bring upon them.** And He did not do it."

Jonah 3:5-10 (AMP)

"For whatsoever things were written aforetime **were written for our learning,** that we through patience and comfort of the scriptures might have hope."

Romans 15:4

"Such things were written in the Scriptures long ago **to teach us.** And the Scriptures give us hope and encouragement as we wait patiently for God's promises to be fulfilled."

Romans 15:4 (NLT)

For *whatever was written in earlier times was written* **for our instruction**, so that through **endurance** and the **encouragement of the Scriptures** we might have hope and overflow with **confidence** in His **promises**.

Romans 15:4 (AMP)

16. The Fasting-Prayer Empowers the Believer for Effective Spiritual Warfare

i. *There's a Spiritual Battle, Fight, Struggle, Warfare:*

Believe it or not, every believer is in a spiritual fight, spiritual battle, spiritual struggle and warfare.

The Bible says,

"FOR WE WRESTLE not against flesh and blood, but *against* principalities, against **powers**, against the *rulers of the darkness* of this world, against *spiritual wickedness* in high places."

Ephesians 6:12

"FOR WE are not FIGHTING AGAINST FLESH-AND-BLOOD ENEMIES, but **against** *evil rulers and authorities of the unseen world, against mighty powers in this dark world*, and against *evil spirits* in the heavenly places."

Ephesians 6:12 (NLT)

"FOR OUR STRUGGLE is NOT AGAINST FLESH AND BLOOD [contending only with physical opponents], but against the rulers, against the powers, **against** the world forces of this [present] darkness, against the spiritual *forces* of wickedness in the heavenly **(supernatural)** *places*."

Ephesians 6:12 (AMP)

"...A LIFE-OR-DEATH FIGHT...*against the DEVIL* and ALL HIS ANGELS."

Ephesians 6:12 (MSG)

ii. *Don't Be Ignorant of Your Enemy's Schemes, Devices and Ways:*

"**Lest Satan** *should get an advantage of us:* for WE ARE NOT IGNORANT *of* his DEVICES."

2 Corinthians 2:11

"to **keep Satan** *from taking advantage of us;* for WE ARE NOT IGNORANT *of* his SCHEMES."

2 Corinthians 2:11 (AMP)

"so that **Satan** *will not outsmart us.* For WE ARE FAMILIAR *with his* EVIL SCHEMES."

2 Corinthians 2:11 (NLT)

"After all, we don't want to unwittingly give **Satan** an opening for yet more mischief—WE'RE NOT OBLIVIOUS to *his* SLY WAYS!"

2 Corinthians 2:11 (MSG)

iii. God Has Given Us Spiritual Armour and Weapons of Warfare

God has given each believer weapons to use against the forces of darkness and invisible powers of the devil. (2 Corinthians 10:3-5)

Put on the whole Armour of God

The Scriptures enjoin us to:

"PUT ON THE WHOLE ARMOUR of GOD, that ye may be able to stand against the wiles of the devil. For we wrestle not against flesh and blood, but against principalities, against powers, against the rulers of the darkness of this world, against spiritual wickedness in high places.

Wherefore take unto you the whole armour of God, that ye may be able to withstand in the evil day, and having done all, to stand.

Stand therefore, having your loins girt about with truth, and having on the **breastplate of**

righteousness; And your feet shod with the preparation of the **gospel of peace**;

Above all, taking the **shield of faith**, wherewith ye shall be able to quench all the fiery darts of the wicked.

And take **the helmet of salvation**, and **the sword of the Spirit**, which is **the word of God**: PRAYING ALWAYS WITH ALL PRAYER and supplication *IN THE SPIRIT…"*

Ephesians 6:10-18

Use Your Weapons of Warfare

"For ***though we walk in the flesh, we do not war after the flesh***: (For the weapons of our warfare **are not carnal**, but **mighty through God** to the *pulling down of strong holds); casting down imaginations*, and every high thing that exalteth itself against the knowledge of God, and *bringing into captivity* every thought to the obedience of Christ"

2 Corinthians 10:3-5

"For **though we walk in the flesh** [as mortal men], **we are NOT carrying on our [spiritual] warfare according to the flesh** *and* **using the weapons of man. THE weapons of our warfare are not physical** [weapons of flesh and blood]. **Our weapons are divinely powerful for the** *destruction of fortresses.*

We are *destroying sophisticated arguments* and every exalted *and* proud thing that sets itself up against the [true] knowledge of God, and we are *taking every thought and purpose captive* to the obedience of Christ"

2 Corinthians 10:3-5 (AMP)

"We are human, **but we don't wage war as humans do**. We use God's mighty weapons, not worldly weapons, *to knock down the strongholds* of human reasoning and *to destroy* false arguments. *We destroy* every proud obstacle that keeps people from knowing God. *We capture* their rebellious thoughts and teach them to obey Christ."

2 Corinthians 10:3-5 (NLT)

- Our Lord Jesus employed the fasting-prayer. He rebuked and cast out demons, healed and delivered many people from demonically influenced conditions during His ministry on earth.
- The prophets of old and Servants of God in the Old Testament used it.

- The Apostles and disciples of the New Testament church employed the useful services of the fasting-prayer.
- Believers, Missionaries, Evangelists, Apostles, Pastors, Bible Teachers, genuine Prophets of God and Church Leaders of the earlier centuries experienced the blessings of the fasting-prayer.

Why should any person remain subject to the devil's fiery darts, schemes, wiles and agenda by neglecting the blessed privilege of employing the fasting-prayer?

17. We Wait Upon and For the Lord through Fasting and Prayer for Him to Incline to Us.

"I *WAITED* patiently and expectantly FOR THE LORD, And HE INCLINED TO ME and HEARD MY CRY"

Psalm 40:1 (AMP)

The word ***incline*** here means, to be favourably disposed towards a person or to be willing and ready to do something for someone.

"I WAITED patiently *for* THE LORD *to* HELP ME, and *He turned to me* and HEARD MY CRY."

Psalm 40:1 (NLT)

- Employing the fasting-prayer releases heavenly attention and divine help as the Lord gives ear to your cry for help concerning anything, everything and all things that concern your life, family, ministry, community, nation; spiritually, physically and financially.

"I WAITED and WAITED and WAITED for God. At last *He looked;* finally *He listened.*"
Psalm 40:1 (MSG)

- When we wait for and upon the Lord through the fasting-prayer, He looks upon us with mercy, in compassion, kindness, goodness and answers are released to meet the needs and concerns of our lives and the work of the Lord to which we are committed.

18. For God to Bring Us Out of Horrible Pits and Out of the Miry Clay

"*I WAITED* **for the** *LORD, and…****He drew me up*** *OUT OF A HORRIBLE PIT – a pit of tumult and of destruction… OUT OF THE MIRY CLAY (froth and slim)*"
Psalm 40:2 (AMP)

- The **horrible pit** and the miry clay here refer to every **unpleasant** and **undesirable** condition, situation and circumstance of life that you may find yourself in. These are conditions of stagnation, hopelessness, helplessness, lack of progress and retrogression.

- As you employ the fasting-prayer during those moments of trouble, trials, temptations, tension, torture, false accusation, condemnation, humiliation, abuse and frustration, the God of heaven will draw you up and bring you out of them, in the mighty name of Jesus.

Case Study: Esther, Mordecai and the Jews (Esther Chapter 2-10).

- Our Lord Jesus Christ was one innocent individual who experienced every form, shape and stage of horrible pit and miry clay situation when He walked the face of this very earth fully as a human being, born of the Virgin Mary, more than 2 thousand years ago, yet He endured and emerged victorious.

Jesus bore in His own body the terrible curse of our sin on the Cross of Calvary.

- He was cast down like a prisoner in a deep, dark, fearful dungeon where He was humiliated, beaten, spat upon, and finally laid down His precious life for us, was crucified on the Cross, and He cried out to God the Father, saying, 'My God, My God, why has Thou Forsaken Me?'

However, after 3 days in the horrible pit of the grave, the Father inclined to Jesus, heard His cry, and drew Him up out of the pit and the miry clay through the resurrection power of the Holy Spirit. God Almighty made Him to ascend from all these abasement.

- Jesus retraced His steps from all the deep anguish into which He had been cast as our substitute, therefore, He will not fail to bring you out, lift you up, and liberate you from your much lighter challenges and tests which will soon become great testimonies in your life.
- The **miry** is something wet and soggy, or covered with mud. **The miry clay** paints the picture of a situation where you suffer. On a slimy, slippery clay, it seems as though

you cannot find a foothold in certain areas of your life, you feel unsteady and you keep slipping and sinking.

You may be experiencing misery after misery, feeling the absence of the peace of God, the comfort of the Holy Spirit, and see only the presence of sorrow. However, there is hope and good news for you.

- As you employ the fasting-prayer, our beloved Redeemer will release divine help into your life as He did for **Joseph** – *the son of Jacob*, who suffered from the **PIT**, down to **PORTIPHAR'S HOUSE**, then to **PRISON**, but, God lifted him up and brought him out of the PRISON to the **PALACE** where he became **PRIME MINISTER** (Genesis 37:40-50).

PRAYER: I pray for you, from today, may you be lifted from every spiritual, physical and financial pit and prison-like condition to your high places of destiny, in the mighty name of Jesus, Amen!

19. For God to Set Your Feet Upon a Rock and Establish Your Steps

"I WAITED...for the LORD, and He...SET MY FEET UPON A ROCK, steadying my footsteps *and* ESTABLISHING my path."

Psalm 40:1, 2 (AMP)

- Employing the fasting-prayer releases the power of God for completeness in your life.
- The Lord will cause you to be deeply rooted and firmly grounded in every area of your life and ministry.
- You will experience the firm ground of divine accomplishment.
- Failure becomes a thing of the past in your life.
- The glory of God will be released in all that you do as was the case for Joseph – the son of Jacob.
- The peace of God and the comfort of the Holy Spirit become your portion.

Just as **Joseph** – *the son of Jacob*, was delivered from the *PIT*, through *PORTIPHAR'S HOUSE*, to the *PRISON* and then to the *PALACE* to become *PRIME MINISTER* and Lord of all in Egypt, so our Lord JESUS CHRIST - the true LORD of ALL, will make you rule and reign over every situation and circumstance in your life, family and ministry by divine establishment.

PRAYER: *I pray for you now, in the name of Jesus Christ, if you are cast into any form of lowest pit of shame, sorrow and sadness, like*

> *Joseph – son of Jacob, may the power of God release you now, and may you be lifted up to stand on the same elevated, firm, solid, sure, and everlasting rock of divine favour, by the power of the Holy Spirit, Amen!*

As the Lord set your feet upon a rock, He will establish your paths in life – in your health, in your education and career, in your marriage-relationship and family-life, in your business/projects and investments, in your ministry, and everything that concerns you. Your story is changing now!

Case Study:
Hannah - the barren woman, became mother of seven children (1 Samuel 1:20; 2:5).

20. For God to Put a New Song in Your Mouth

"I WAITED…for the LORD…HE PUT A NEW SONG in MY MOUTH, A SONG of PRAISE to OUR GOD; Many will see and fear [with great reverence] And will trust confidently in the Lord."

Psalm 40:1, 3 (AMP)

- By employing the fasting-prayer, the power of God works on your behalf and supernaturally changes your story.

- A change of story leads to a corresponding change of prayer points, which then leads to a change of song – a Song of Victory (SOV).

- If you have been asking God to lead you to find your God-ordained wife or husband in marriage, you will now thank God for giving you a wife or husband.

- If you have been asking God for a child, you will now thank Him for the blessing of a child.

- If you have been asking God for a job, career, business, immigration settlement, ministry, financial breakthrough and blessings of any kind; your prayer will now change from asking to thanking Him for His blessings in your life which will also increase your level of commitment to the things of God.

PRAYER: *I pray for you in the precious name of Jesus, from today, your story will change as you employ the fasting-prayer and seek the face of the Lord fervently.*

"HE *has* GIVEN ME A NEW SONG *to* SING, a hymn of praise to our God. Many will see what He has done and be amazed. They will put their trust in the Lord."

Psalm 40:3 (NLT)

Case Study:

The above was the transformed story of Hannah, the barren woman, after she employed the fasting-prayer. Her life was changed, her prayer points changed, her life was blessed, and she sang a new song unto the Lord.

(**For further Study**, Read: 1 Samuel 1:1-28, *especially* verses 2, 7, 8, 10-12; also, read **1 Samuel 2:1-10** for Hannah's New Prayer Points, New Song of Praise to God).

21. For God to Renew Your Strength Spiritually and Physically.

"But THEY THAT WAIT UPON THE LORD SHALL RENEW THEIR STRENGTH; they shall mount up with **wings as eagles**; they shall **run, and not be weary**; and they shall **walk, and not faint**."

Isaiah 40:31

- Waiting upon the Lord as in our scripture above refers to seeking the face of the Lord through fasting and prayer.

- There is a supernatural manifestation during the period of biblical fasting and prayer whereby the power and strength of Jehovah is released into every area of spiritual, physical, emotional, mental and psychological weakness in the life of those who spend the time to wait upon the Lord.

- During this spiritual exercise, power changes hand, sicknesses, diseases and infirmities give way to divine health. All weak, inactive, dysfunctional and broken organs of the human body are visited by the Balm of Gilead.

- The anointing of the Holy Spirit refreshes, renews, rebuilds and revives every element of the body to prepare it to be more able to be offered as a living sacrifice to the Lord in reasonable service to the Kingdom of God.

"But **those who** WAIT upon God GET FRESH STRENGTH. They *spread their wings* and soar like eagles, **They** *run* and DON'T GET TIRED, they *walk* and DON'T LAG BEHIND."

Isaiah 40:31 (MSG)

The purpose of this kingdom blessing is to be more readily active in working for the Lord, running errands for King Jesus without complaining or making excuses, because we know that He alone is the source of our life and our strength.

As we employ the fasting-prayer in waiting upon the Lord, He will cause us to:

- Be *renewed* and *refreshed* in strength spiritually and physically.
- Mount up with *wings* like eagles.
- Run and *not be weary*.
- Walk and *not faint*.

Such spiritual and physical strength and blessings are received by waiting upon the Lord with expectancy, trusting and hoping in Him for change of position, circumstance and renewal.

22. For God to Hear Us From Heaven, Forgive Our Sins & Heal Our Land

"and My people, who are called by My Name, HUMBLE THEMSELVES, and PRAY and SEEK **(crave, require as a necessity)** MY FACE and turn from their wicked ways, then I WILL HEAR [them] FROM HEAVEN, and FORGIVE THEIR SIN and HEAL THEIR LAND."

2 Chronicles 7:14 (AMP)

- This is a conditional covenant promise from the covenant-keeping God in relation to biblical fasting and prayer.

The Lord says,

"Then if My people who are called by My name will *humble themselves* and *pray* and *seek My face and turn from their wicked ways*, **I will hear from heaven** and **will forgive their sins** and RESTORE THEIR LAND."

2 Chronicles 7:14 (NLT)

When we Employ the biblical fasting-prayer, it will open up for us:

i. Heavenly Answers to Prayer - ***I will hear from heaven*** (vs. 14)

ii. Forgiveness of Sins – *I will forgive their sins* (vs. 14).

iii. Divine Healing and Restoration – ***I will heal their land*** (vs. 14).

"and my people, my God-defined people, respond by humbling themselves, praying, seeking my presence, and turning their backs on their wicked lives, *I'll be there ready for you:* **I'll LISTEN *from heaven*, FORGIVE *their sins*, *and RESTORE their land to* HEALTH.**"

2 Chronicles 7:14 (MSG)

It takes biblical fasting and prayer to release the above destiny-fulfilling blessings into a person's life, family, ministry and nation.

23. For Transformation of Our Lives, For God to Move through us & Work Through Us to Fulfill His Glorious Purposes on Earth

Jesus emphatically said,

"...***this kind*** *does not go out* **except by** *PRAYER AND FASTING"*

Matthew 17:21 (NKJV)

- **Esther's** life was transformed, moved by God and used greatly to fulfil God's purpose for the Jews in her generation.
- **Ezra's** life was used mightily by God to fulfil Kingdom purposes in the lives of God's people and the nation during his time.
- **Nehemiah's** heart was moved by God and he availed himself for the Lord to use him gloriously for the rebuilding of Jerusalem.

PRAYER: May the Lord transform our lives, move through us and use us as *the Esthers, the Ezras* and *the Nehemiahs* of our generation to fulfil His glorious purposes in our families, communities, work-places, churches, schools/colleges/universities and our nations, in the powerful name of Jesus Christ, Amen!

15

How Long Should a Person Fast?

Since fasting is a time set apart to be before God, the duration should be determined by our relationship with God; for whatever reason you are going before Him.

There is no hard and fast rule about how long anybody should fast for.

Meanwhile, the following may be considered:

- One should Pray to the Lord and seek Guidance on the length of the fast beforehand.

- Keep your promises with the Lord. Try not to break your fast half-way, unless you are led by the Holy Spirit to do so.

- If you decide and plan to fast for any number of days, do it unto the Lord. If you eat nothing for 24 hours, it is a day's fast as you wait upon the Lord. In the same way, if you abstain from food to be with the Lord in prayer for 72 hours, it is a (3) three day fast.

- Another thing that should influence the length of the fasting is your need and desperation.

- A person can plan to fast until there is an assurance of victory or until results come – if such a person has a mountain to remove. So, the length of the fast may be determined by your burden for unsaved souls in your family, work-place, neighbourhood or community, or your burden to see someone delivered from sin, sickness, suffering or suppression.

- However, the duration of a fast may be as long as 40 days.

- The duration of a fast can also be as brief and short as a single day - 24 hours, as in the case of David and Israel, recorded in (2 Samuel 1:11-12).

- Jesus Christ fasted 40 days and nights (Matthew 4:1-2)

- Moses fasted for 40 days and 40 nights (Exodus 34:28; Deut. 9:18-21)
- Elijah fasted for 40 days and nights (1 Kings 19:8)
- Daniel fasted for 21 days [3 weeks] - (Daniel 10:3)
- Esther, Mordecai and the Jews Fasted for 3 days and nights (Esther 4:16)

All these were of God's leading and direction of which one must be carefully led.

16

How to Start Your Fasting

*"Physical exercise has **some value**, but **SPIRITUAL EXERCISE is VALUABLE in EVERY WAY,** because it promises life both for the present and for the future."*
1 Timothy 4:8 (GNT)

- Every important journey requires special preparation. Fasting is a spiritual journey, so there is the need to prepare spiritually and physically for it.

- Fasting is an important spiritual exercise which calls for special preparation.

- As you prepare yourself to minister to the Lord and to wait upon Him, the Lord also prepares to give you attention, and to minister to you at the point of your needs through His Holy Spirit and through the ministry of His Angels (Matthew 4:11; Acts 13:2).

God Recognizes and Honours Your Preparation to Fast

The Lord promises that,

"...***before they call,*** I will answer; and while they are yet speaking, I will hear."

Isaiah 65:24

"...before they call, I will answer; and ***while they are still speaking, I will hear.***"

Isaiah 65:24 (AMP)

"***I will answer them before they even call to me.*** While they are still talking about **their needs, I will go ahead** and answer their prayers!"

Isaiah 65:24 (NLT)

"Before they call out, I'll answer. Before they've finished speaking, I'll have heard."

Isaiah 65:24 (MSG)

With all these promises and assurances from the Almighty God, your prayer and fasting journey will be very meaningful, interesting, enjoyable and worth the while.

1. Every fast must be dedicated to the Lord.
2. For a fast of 2 weeks or more, it is helpful to withdraw from other things, go some place alone to rest and give oneself to prayer, praise, worship and the reading of the Word of God. Jesus Christ is our perfect example, He withdrew into the wilderness during His 40 days fasting preceding His public Ministry as He was led by the Holy Spirit.
3. A pleasant, restful, peaceful atmosphere should be sought for the purpose of our fasting, this will enable us to give undivided attention to God and reap the full blessings of waiting upon the Lord.
4. Start reducing your food-intake as the day of the fasting approaches. Where possible, eat only fresh fruits and/or fresh vegetables for a few days prior to your fasting, to prepare your system and your entire body for this important spiritual "journey".
5. Pure, lukewarm drinking water should be made available in abundance for drinking- in the case of normal fast (fasting without food, but with water). Avoid drinking cold or iced water during fasting. It is helpful to drink lukewarm water when fasting.

6. It is good to take warm bath during the fast because the body will start to eliminate certain gases through the pores of our skin.
7. Most of the time, you may experience some strange odour/odor/ scent/ smell during your fasting, and you may sometimes become unbearable to others. When this happens, do not worry, your body is simply going through a vital cleansing period which is good for your health and you will be healed of certain diseases. Spiritual and physical healing occurs during fasting. However, as much as possible, do your best to maintain good personal hygiene.
8. Have an objective and an aim for your fasting. Be purposeful. Be intentional. Fasting without an aim is like traveling to an unknown destination, or stepping out of your house to the Town Centre aimlessly.
9. Prepare your mind to:
    - Pray,
    - Read and Study the Word of God,
    - Worship and Praise God,
    - Hear from the Holy Spirit,
    - Learn new things from the Lord,
    - Receive from God.

10. Have a strong desire to draw closer to God through Prayer, the Word of God, Worship, among other things, and be in readiness to "flow" as the Holy Spirit leads you. Sometimes, we may set ourselves some number of days to fast, whereby God may not have finished with us, so, we may need to follow the leading of the Holy Spirit all through.

17

Basic Ingredients of Biblical Fasting

Fasting without engaging in the following will render your fast unbiblical and ineffective. For maximum effectiveness of your fast, the following ingredients should be part of your fasting.

Biblical Fasting is Accompanied By:

1. Earnest Prayer

(Ezra 8:23; Nehemiah 1:4; Psalm 35:13; Daniel 9:3; Luke 5:33; II Chronicles 7:14; James 5:16b-18; Isaiah 58:6, 9).

- **Moses** prayed earnestly during his fast and received answers (Deuteronomy 9:20, 24-29).

- **Ezra** and the Israelite captives entreated God in prayer during their fast. They had tremendous results (Ezra 8:23).
- **Hannah** prayed earnestly to God during her fast. She became the mother of a Prophet, Samuel, and mother of seven children (1 Samuel 1:10-12, 15, 17, 19-20; 1 Samuel 2:5).
- **Jesus** started His public ministry with prayer and ended with prayer on the Cross of Calvary (Luke 3:21-22; Matthew 4:1-2; Luke 23:46).
- As you give yourself to prayer during the fast, the power of God will change your whole life, it will refresh you, renew you and build you up into a more fruitful vessel for the Lord Jesus Christ (2 Timothy 2:19-24).
- The fasting-prayer defeats unbelief in your heart and builds a strong faith in you to claim the promises of God (Mark 11:22-24).
- Churches and congregations which fast and pray will experience growth and see the power of the Holy Spirit move mightily with miracles, healing and deliverance in the midst (Acts 13:1-3).

- A chain of fasting and intercessory prayers will set *Fellowships ablaze* to move out and reach out for God in the power of the Holy Spirit (Acts 13:1-3).
- Spend time praying for others during fasting (1 Timothy 2:1-5).
- Pray and tell God the desires of your heart, He will grant them according to His perfect will for your life (Psalm 37:4-5).

2. Humility

(Deuteronomy 9:18; Psalm 69:10; 1 Kings 21:27; Nehemiah 9:1).

David, the sweet Psalmist said,

But as for me, when they were sick, My clothing was sackcloth; *I HUMBLED MYSELF WITH FASTING…"*

Psalm 35:13 (NKJV)

"But as for me, when they were sick, my clothing was sackcloth (mourning garment); I HUMBLED MY SOUL WITH FASTING, And I prayed with my head bowed on my chest."

Psalm 35:13 (AMP)

3. Personal Heart Searching, Repentance and Confession of Sin

(1 Samuel 7:6; Nehemiah 9:1-3; Psalm 139:23-24)

David prayed,

"**Search** me, (thoroughly), O God, and **known my heart**! Try me and know my thoughts! And see if there is any wicked or hurtful way in me, and lead me in the way everlasting."

Psalm 139:23-24 (AMP)

- Sincerely search your heart and your life through personal self-examination. Consider how you have lived your life these past years in relation to the Word of God.
- Consider your Relationships.

i. **Your Vertical Relationship** – that is your personal relationship with God, your heavenly Father.

ii. **Your Horizontal Relationship** – that is your relationship with people on this earth – your spouse, your children, your in-laws, people in your family, people at the place of work, people in church, people in your neighbourhood and community, people in school/ college/ university, people in hospitals, people you meet on the bus/ train/tram or in the street.

- Check your past hidden and secret sins; People you may have locked up in your heart as a result of offences and bitterness without forgiving them; and People you may have cursed in your heart and with your mouth.

- Examine yourself. Repent of all evil and wicked ways. Return to Gods ways and He will Forgive you, Restore you and Establish you. Fear not!

4. **Read, Study, Memorize & Meditate on the Word of God**

(Nehemiah 9:1-3; Jeremiah 36:6; 36:10).

Job said,

*"**I have NOT** departed from the **commandment of His lips;** I have **treasured the Words** of His mouth **more than my necessary food**"*

Job 23:12 (NKJV)

"I HAVE not departed from His commands, but have TREASURED HIS WORDS MORE THAN DAILY FOOD."

Job 23:12 (NLT)

I've obeyed EVERY WORD HE'S SPOKEN, and not just obeyed His advice—*I've treasured it.*

Job 23:12 (MSG)

- Read and study the Word of God. Meditating on the Word of God keeps us close to God, establishes us in His promises and builds the mind of Christ in us more and more, then we begin to grow stronger, to stand more firmly and soar higher in the power of His might. As you fast, your mind becomes clearer for Bible study.

    Read and fellowship with the scriptures for deeper insight into the value of the Word of God. *(Psalm 19:8, Psalm 119:25, 28, 92-93, 97-105, 1 Peter 2:1-2, Hebrews 5:12-4)*

- You could take one book of the Bible and study it during fasting, for example, *Jonah chapter 1- 4, Ezra chapter 1-10, and Esther chapter 1-10.*

- You could also do a Word Study, Topical Study or Character Study.

- Memorize Scriptures and use them in your prayers, such as, *Luke 1:37; Genesis 18:14, Psalm 34:7, Job 42:1-2, Psalm 127:1, Psalm 121:1-2.*

- God respects and honours His word. God's word in your mouth is as powerful as His Word in His own mouth.

5. Abstain from Sex by Mutual Consent with Your Spouse Only for the Purpose and Period of Fasting & Prayer

The Bible says,

*"Do not deprive one another **except with consent for a time, that you may give yourselves to fasting and prayer;** and come together again so that Satan does not tempt you because of your lack of self-control."*

1 Corinthians 7:5 (NKJV)

6. Sing Psalms, Hymns, Songs of Praise and Worship God

(Nehemiah 9:1-3, Psalm 92:1, John 4:23-24)

The song of the righteous is a prayer unto the Father in heaven and will be answered with a blessing.

The Scriptures say,

*"**Let the** [spoken] **word of Christ** have its home within you **[dwelling in your heart and mind**—permeating every aspect of your being] as you teach [spiritual things] and admonish and train one another with all wisdom, singing psalms and hymns and spiritual songs with thankfulness in your hearts to God."*

Colossians 3:16 (AMP)

7. Make Time for Rest

And Jesus said to them,

"…Come aside by yourselves to a deserted place and REST A WHILE…"

Mark 6:31 (NKJV)

As you relax your body during fasting, your mind will be refreshed and the Lord will reveal Himself to you and open up to you His Glorious treasures.

8. Personal Demeanour

Jesus said,

*"…**when you fast, comb your hair and wash your face.** Then no one will notice that you are fasting, except your Father, who knows what you do in private. **And your Father, who sees everything, will reward you.**"*

Matthew 6:17 (NLT)

"If you 'go into training' inwardly, act normal outwardly. **Shampoo and comb your hair, brush your teeth, wash your face.** God doesn't require attention-getting devices. He won't overlook what you are doing; He'll reward you well."

Matthew 6:17-18 (MSG)

9. Weeping

(2 Samuel 1:12; Nehemiah 1:4; Esther 4:3; Psalm 69:10)

*"Therefore also now, saith the Lord, TURN ye even **to Me with all your heart**, and WITH FASTING, and WITH WEEPING, and with mourning"*

Joel 2:12

18

The Wrong Kind of Fasting
(Isaiah 58:1-5, Matthew 6:16-18, Ecclesiastes 3:1-11)

The wrong kind of fasting refers to a fast that does not please the Almighty God. There were times in my early Christian life when I fasted ignorantly without engaging with the relevant aspects of biblical fasting – spending quality time in the presence of the Lord in prayer, reading and study of the Word of God, worship, praises and listening to the Lord. It is the **Wrong Concept of Biblical Fasting**.

In the book of the Prophet Isaiah, these questions are asked,

"Wherefore have we fasted, say they, and thou seest not?

Wherefore have we afflicted our soul, and *thou takest no knowledge? Behold, in the day of your fast ye find pleasure,* and exact *all your labours.* Behold, *ye fast for strife* and *debate,* and *to smite with the fist of wickedness:* ye shall not fast as ye do this day, *to make your voice to be heard on high.*

Is it such a fast that I have chosen?

A day for a man to afflict his soul? Is it to bow down his head as a bulrush, and to spread sackcloth and ashes under him?

Wilt thou call this a fast, and an acceptable day to the Lord?

Isaiah 58:3-5

Jesus said,

"And **whenever you are fasting, do not look gloomy like the hypocrites,** for they put on a sad and dismal face [like actors, discolouring their faces with ashes or dirt] so that their fasting may be seen by men. I assure you and most solemnly say to you, they [already] have their reward in full.

But **when you fast,** put oil on your head [as you normally would to groom your hair] and wash your face so that your fasting will not be noticed by people, but by *your Father who is in secret; and your Father who sees [what is done] in secret will reward you.*"

Matthew 6:16-18 (AMP)

To engage in biblical fasting, it is helpful NOT to do the following:

- Fasting without making *quality* time to engage in relevant spiritual exercises is not helpful. (For example, Prayer, Bible reading and study, Praise, Worship etc.)
- Giving oneself to *pleasure* of any kind and in any form (sex, games, football, etc.) during the period of fasting is not helpful spiritually.
- *Occupying* oneself with every kind of work during your fast is not helpful.
- *Indulging* in arguments, contentions and quarreling during your fast is not helpful.
- *Making your voice* to be heard on high for people to know that you are fasting is a hypocritical religious activity. Avoid it.
- Putting on a *sad countenance*, disfiguring one's face to readily appear to people to be fasting goes without reward (Matthew 6:16-18).
- Trying to *impress* others with or by your fasting is not godly. Impress no one, not even your Pastor or church leader. Do it all unto the LORD.

- Keeping oneself busy with unnecessary and unfruitful conversations and gossiping during your fasting is not helpful (Titus 3:9; 2 Timothy 2:23).

19

The Right Kind of Fasting

The right concept of biblical fasting refers to fasting that pleases God in relation to things which should accompany biblical fasting. It is the fast which God chooses.

The Lord says,

"[Rather] *is this not the fast which I choose*, To undo the bonds of wickedness, To tear to pieces the ropes of the yoke, To let the oppressed go free And break apart every [enslaving] yoke? "Is it not to divide your bread with the hungry And bring the homeless poor into the house; When you see the naked, that you cover him, And not to hide yourself from [the needs of] your own flesh *and* blood?"

Isaiah 58:6-7 (AMP)

- Take a good bath or shower, comb/style your hair, dress up and put up a good appearance, not a sad countenance.
- Make your fasting time 'a prayer time' – praying, not only for yourself, but interceding for others as well as for the work of God (1 Timothy 2:1-5).
- Maximize your fasting to loose bonds of wickedness and injustice.
- To undo the heavy burdens and remove obstacles.
- To set the oppressed free and break every yoke of bondage.
- Benevolence – share food with the hungry.
- Helpfulness – provide for the poor and helpless around you.
- Generosity and kindness to be extended to people that the Holy Spirit leads you to minister to.
- Do not fast to impress anybody, not your spouse, or even your Pastor or church leader. Count hypocrisy out.
- Dedicate your fasting unto the Lord and seek His face sincerely and diligently.

- Don't be led by your flesh, be led by the Holy Spirit to keep your vow, time, and agreement with the Lord (Romans 8:14).
- Develop the closest of relationships and fellowships with the Lord through prayer, Bible Study, Praise and Worship.
- You must always *prepare for* and *plan your fasting*.
- Accompany your fasting purposefully with prayer-targets. Set prayer-targets for your fasting.

20

20 Great Lessons In Biblical Fasting

"…is this not the fast which I choose, To undo the bonds of wickedness, To tear to pieces the ropes of the yoke, To let the oppressed go free And break apart every [enslaving] yoke? "Is it not to divide your bread with the hungry And bring the homeless poor into the house; When you see the naked, that you cover him, And not to hide yourself from [the needs of] your own flesh and blood? "Then your light will break out like the dawn, And your healing (restoration, new life) will quickly spring forth; Your righteousness will go before you [leading you to peace and prosperity], The glory of the Lord will be your rear guard. "Then you will call, and the Lord will answer; You will cry for help, and He will say,

'Here I am.' If you take away from your midst the yoke [of oppression], The finger pointed in scorn [toward the oppressed or the godly], and [every form of] wicked (sinful, unjust) speech, And if you offer yourself to [assist] the hungry And satisfy the need of the afflicted, Then your light will rise in darkness And your gloom will become like midday. "And the Lord will continually guide you, And satisfy your soul in scorched and dry places, And give strength to your bones; And you will be like a watered garden, And like a spring of water whose waters do not fail. "And your people will rebuild the ancient ruins; You will raise up and restore the age-old foundations [of buildings that have been laid waste]; You will be called Repairer of the Breach, Restorer of Streets with Dwellings."

Isaiah 58:6-14 (AMP)

1. Through Biblical fasting and prayer, chains and bonds of wickedness are loosed (Isaiah 58:6).
2. Heavy burdens are removed (Isaiah 58:6; *Case Study*: Hannah - 1 Samuel 1 & 2).
3. The oppressed are set free (Isaiah 58:6; *Case Study*: Esther, Mordecai and the Jews)
4. Every kind and every form of yoke is broken through biblical fasting and prayer (Isaiah 58:6; Isaiah 10:27; For Example, Health yokes, financial yokes, marital yoke).

5. *Benevolence*: the hungry are fed and the naked clothed (Isaiah 58:7).
6. The poor are catered for, protected and provided for, through biblical fasting (Isaiah 58:7).
7. *Light Promised:* The light of God will break forth into every area of darkness in your life and family (Isaiah 58:7; John 1:5).
8. *Health Promised:* Healing shall spring forth speedily and quickly into your life – spiritually, physically, emotionally, mentally, psychologically and financially (Isaiah 58:8).
9. The *Glory* and the *beauty of God* plus divine protection will be your portion (Isaiah 58:8).
10. *Answers to prayer* are promised and assured (Isaiah 58:9).
11. *Radiant Lives:* Divine breakthroughs and open doors promised. You will shine like a star. You will be a star in your family. You will be bright with Joy (Isaiah 58:10; Job 11:17; Psalm 34:5; Ecclesiastes 8:1; Daniel 12:3; John 5:35; Acts 6:15; 2 Corinthians 3:18-19; Philippians 2:15; Revelations 21:11).
12. *Divine Guidance Promised:* God's Spirit and God's angels will guide you continually and always (Isaiah 58:11; Psalm 34:7).
13. *Satisfaction* of your needs. God will satisfy your mouth with good things (Isaiah 58:11).

14. *Divine Strength Promised.* God will strengthen you. His Joy will be your strength (Isaiah 58:11).
15. You will be like a *well-watered garden* (Isaiah 58:11; Jeremiah 31:12).
16. You will experience *an unfading life* (Psalm 1:3; Psalm 103; Psalm 92:14; Jeremiah 17:8).
17. *Restoration Promised.* God will forgive your sins and restore you completely (Isaiah 58:12).
18. The *Joy of the Lord* will be your portion in the land of the living (Isaiah 58:14).
19. *Exaltation and Promotion* will come your way from above (Psalm 75:6; Deuteronomy 26:19; Deuteronomy 28:1,13; Isaiah 49:23; Isaiah 60:14).
20. *Inheritance and heritage* promised you (Isaiah 58:14; Leviticus 20:24; Deuteronomy 1:28; Joshua 24:28).

21

Who Should Fast?

Jesus said,

"...**WHEN YOU FAST,** do not be like the hypocrites... But you, **WHEN YOU FAST**, anoint your head and wash your face...and your Father who sees in secret will reward you openly"

Matthew 6:16-18 (NKJV)

- Fasting is a spiritual exercise for all believers. It strengthens the believer's faith and enhances growth and maturity in Christ.

- According to the word of God, fasting is the privilege of every child of God (Matthew 6:16-18; 2 Chronicles 7:14).

- Jesus fasted, and He gave us a teaching on the principles of fasting. This is because He expects His followers to fast and pray (Luke 4:1-3; Matthew 6:16-18).

- I think that no Christian is too old or too sick to fast and pray. This is because as a result of biblical fasting, your strength will be renewed by God and your body will be healed of sicknesses and all kinds of diseases. Every believer can, and should fast.

The Scriptures say,

I can do all things [which He has called me to do] **through Him who strengthens and empowers me** [to fulfill His purpose—I am self-sufficient in Christ's sufficiency; I am ready for anything and equal to anything through **Him who infuses me with inner strength** and confident peace.]

Philippians 4:13 (AMP)

- When you fast, you reap the Spiritual Promises, Benefits and Blessings of fasting in accordance with God's Holy Word (Galatians 6:7-9).

- Learn more about Apostle Paul's fasted life. He fasted often. Fasting is a way of ministering unto the Lord (2 Corinthians 11:27; Acts 9:9; Acts 13:2-3).
- Fasting strengthens our faith in believing God for the fulfillment of His promises for our lives on earth (Hebrews 11:6).
- Fasting is an important Spiritual exercise that helps us put our body into subjection and yielded to God in holiness and purity, and for the Holy Spirit to use us ultimately to fulfil God's purposes on earth (1 Corinthians 9:27).

You can also **"Sanctify a fast…"** (Joel 1:14-15)

22

How to Break Your Fast

"Then Jesus was led up by the Spirit into the wilderness...He had **fasted forty days** and **forty nights**, afterward He was **hungry**." (Matthew 4:1-2)

- Discipline yourself, keep your promise with God by fasting the full length of days or weeks He has shown you to observe in waiting upon Him.

- The normal time to break your fast with food at the end of it all is when you naturally feel hungry.

- Natural hunger returned to Jesus after he had fasted 40 days and nights (Matthew 4:2, Luke 4:1-3)

Jesus prepared for the Test by fasting forty days and forty nights. That left Him, of course, in a state of extreme hunger, which the Devil took advantage of in the first test: "Since You are God's Son, speak the word that will turn these stones into loaves of bread." (MSG)

"***After*** *spending forty days and nights without food,* ***Jesus was hungry***.*"*

Matthew 4:2 (GNT)

"**After** He had gone without food for forty days and forty nights, He became hungry."

Matthew 4:2 (AMP)

It is important to note that, the main reason the human stomach reacts violently when it is denied food for some hours or a day or two is due to the usual habit of eating, being fed and filled continually.

- After a period of fasting, hunger naturally returns. After your fast, you must eat when hunger returns, otherwise your body will enter into a starvation period.
- If you have a short fast of a few days, it is helpful to break your fast, *first*, with warm water, some hot drink, then fresh fruits and vegetables.
- If it is a long fast of weeks, it is helpful to break your fast gradually with fresh fruits,

fresh vegetables, then followed by your main meal taken in light quantities.
- The longer you fast, the slower you should break your fast, in order to maintain good health, and avoid any health damages to your body after fasting.
- Sometimes, the desire to eat soon after your fasting may be very strong, however, we must be careful *not to over-eat*, especially the first day.
- It is helpful *not to* break a long fast with heavy meat, sweets, bread, etc. for good health's sake.
- You may maintain normal weight and naturally add many healthy years to your lifespan if you break a long fast with fresh fruits and fresh vegetables.
(Consider – 1 Corinthians 3:16, 1 Corinthians 6:19-20, 1 Corinthians 11:30).
- Do not break your fast *all of a sudden with a heavy meal*. That can disturb your body and affect your good health.

Great blessings await you. Please break your fast wisely.

God bless you!

Bibliography

- Hymn – What a Friend We Have in Jesus: *https://reasonabletheology.org/hymn-story-friend-jesus/*
- http://staugustine.com/living/religion/2015-04-23/story-behind-song-what-friend-we-have-jesus

Other Books by the Author

About the Author

Revd. Christian Damanka is an ordained Minister of the Gospel, called as a Pastor and Bible Teacher in the Body of Christ. He's a well-groomed member of Scripture Union (SU), Youth For Christ (YFC) and Full Gospel Business Men's Fellowship International (FGBMFI). Revd. Damanka served as the pioneer and Pastor of House of Faith Ministries (World Missions Church) in London, UK, for over 13 years.

He presently serves as Founder and Director of Missions for ANCC UK, (House of Prayer), Destiny Centre. As a Purpose-driven servant of God with a message of HOPE for his generation, Revd. Damanka believes that God has a unique plan of excellence for everyone who is 'willing and obedient'.

As a UK qualified Teacher and accredited Trainer, he's also taught in Secondary Schools and Colleges in London. He is currently a permanent Lecturing Staff of Newham College of Further Education, London, UK.

As a professional and a practitioner, Revd. Damanka is a registered member of UK Board of Healthcare Chaplaincy (UKBHC), a member of the

College of Health Care Chaplains (CHCC), and a member of the Society for Education and Training (SET), UK.

He holds a Master of Arts (MA) in Biblical Counselling from Trinity South West University, USA; studied Missional Leadership at Masters Level with the University of Wales, UK; a Bachelor of Theology (BTh) from South London Christian College (SLCC); and a Postgraduate Certificate in Healthcare Chaplaincy from London South Bank University.

Revd. Damanka also holds a Level 7 in EDSML and provides training in Leadership, Strategic Management and short courses in Health and Social Care, Childcare and Education.

He is a Prayer-loving man, a counsellor, youth mentor, radio evangelist, a gifted singer, a prolific writer and author of 5 best-selling books including:

i. **How Can I Know the Will of God?**
ii. **Women- Vessels of Honour**
iii. **Unravelling the Secrets of the Fear of God** *(Fulfilling the Whole Duty of Man)*
iv. **33 Blessings & Benefits of the Fear of God.**

www.ingramcontent.com/pod-product-compliance
Lightning Source LLC
Chambersburg PA
CBHW071559080526
44588CB00010B/958